salmonpoetry

This poem presumes the existence of Michelangelo,
of myself, and of a reader.
All else is imagination, sometimes delusion.

The Sistine Gaze

I too begin with scaffolding

A POEM IN THIRTY-ONE MOVEMENTS

BOOKS 1-3
CREATION
ETERNAL DAY
STANDING ON THE WALL

SEAMUS CASHMAN

salmonpoetry

Published in 2015 by
Salmon Poetry
Cliffs of Moher, County Clare, Ireland
Website: www.salmonpoetry.com
Email: info@salmonpoetry.com

ISBN 978-1-910669-06-8

FRONT COVER IMAGE: Sistine Ceiling, detail: female figure in a pseudo-architec-
tural spandrel above the Jesse–David-Saloman [Soloman] lunette.
BACK COVER IMAGE: Back cover image: 'Extrusions' by Seamus Cashman.
COVER DESIGN & TYPESETTING: *Siobhán Hutson*
Printed in Ireland by Sprint Print

Salmon Poetry gratefully acknowledges the support of
The Arts Council / An Chomhairle Ealaoín

Contents

BOOK 2 — ETERNAL DAY — THE WORK
(Verses 117-205)

BOOK 3 — STANDING ON THE WALL
(verses 206–258)

The Sistine Gaze

A POEM IN THIRTY-ONE MOVEMENTS

TO THE READER

My eyes return time and again to one image. It is of a woman in a green jacket, hunkered in a white triangular frame. Her eyes hold mine, and the word 'gaze' slips into my mind. As I stare she seems to invite me to converse. After about forty minutes, soaked in colour downflows, I go along the bustling floor and through the conversation hum—eying all the faces tuned to the high ceiling—to exit the Sistine Chapel.

Before leaving the Vatican, I climb the five hundred or more steps to the top of Michelangelo's great basilica dome. Just to sense an edge or boundary, to settle.

This visit to the Sistine was for the art, aware of its recent cleaning and restoration, but also to nostalgically reconnect with a brief casual visit I had made decades earlier. Since that first visit, the then sombre darkness of the ceiling imagery had remained my most persistent recollection.

Readers who have not seen the Sistine Chapel, or know little about it will find a brief outline of the content of Michelangelo's frescoes as an appendix to this introductory note. Essentially a song of creation, embellished and informed by biblical and other Judaic traditions, the 'ceiling' is Michelangelo's masterwork, bridging 'different faiths, cultures, eras, and sexualities'[1] and celebrating the human body. However, on completing it in October 1512, the artist wrote in anger to a friend:

> Here they make helmets and swords from chalices
> and by the handful sell the blood of Christ;
> his cross and thorns are made into lances and shields;
> yet even Christ's patience still rains down.

But let him come no more to these parts;
his blood would rise up as far as the stars;
since now in Rome his flesh is being sold;
and every road to virtue is closed. [2]

A second commission, 'The Last Judgement', unveiled on
the west gable altar wall twenty-nine years later, completes
the crossing, bringing humanity to its magnificent
apocalyptic end. This single fresco is gigantic – some forty-
six feet in height by forty-three wide. All is dramatic
movement involving close to four hundred active naked
figures, some with genitals covered by an offended church
in the 1560s and after. Painted as it were on a non-existent
wall, for there is no frame here, the illusion of the Second
Coming materialises in space before each viewer.

Among all the riches of ceiling and wall, it was a modest
female figure hunkered in a white pseudo-architectural
triangular frame that drew and held my attention. My
'Prologue' to the poem describes her meditative presence.
The word 'gaze' gave me access and a concept, and as
mentioned, the figure seemed to dare me to converse.
Months later back in Dublin, conversation began in the
form of this poem.

Seamus Cashman
10 July 2014

NOTES
1. Blech and Doliner, *The Sistine Secrets*, JR Books, 2008
2. Saslow, trans.. *The Poetry of Michelangelo: an annotated translation*. Yale
U.P., 1991. The sonnet continues:

If ever I wished to shed my worldly treasures,
since no work is left me here, the man in the cope
can do as Medusa did in Mauretania.
   But even if poverty's welcomed up in heaven,
How can we earn the great reward of our state
If another banner weakens that other life? …

LOOKING AT THE
SISTINE FRESCOES

'The Sistine Ceiling' was painted between May 1508 and October 1512. 'The Last Judgement' fresco was undertaken twenty-three years later, from 1535 to 31 October 1541. Michelangelo di Lodovico Buonarroti Simoni (6 March 1475 – 18 February 1564) is buried in the Basilica di Santa Croce in Florence.

Unusually, the Sistine Chapel altar is positioned at the west end of the chapel, not its east gable. On the ceiling, some sixty feet above floor level, are nine central panels which narrate biblical creation stories in reverse 'chronology' (the sequence as painted by Michelangelo), from entrance door to altar.

These nine scenes illustrate: the drunkenness of Noah; the Flood; Noah's sacrifice; Adam & Eve's temptation in the garden and expulsion; the creation of Eve; the creation of Adam; the separation of land and sea; the creation of sun, moon and vegetation; and the separation of light from darkness).

This narrative is 'supported' in the firmament by a troop of twenty seated '*ignudi*', naked young men, sculptural, delicately fleshed, in varied dramatic poses, with unifying ribbons and garlands of flowers.

Beneath those young men is a series of billowy seated portraits of seven prophets and five sibyls – all but one (Jonah) reading books or scrolls. These are by far the largest figures on the ceiling, all some twelve feet high. In between them, flows a sequence of images of 'ancestors of Christ' in mainly family groups with a prominent mother figure in their foregrounds, in home and work settings, wearing stylish, colourful clothes: they represent the forty generations from Abraham to Christ.

Each corner image reveals a tale of death and trauma: David & Goliath; Judith & Holofernes; the Brazen Serpent; the Crucifixion of Haman.

A prophet sits at each gable end: Zacharias above the entrance door; and observing the entire of creation, a rebellious Prometheus-like Jonah in loincloth and vest, his legs overhanging the altar.

Many decorative and structural elements energise the in-between spaces: pairs of children; putti figures; horned ram skulls; bronzed nude symmetrical pairs of sometimes demonic figures; and large bronzed medallions narrating battle tales from the old testament; all filling architectural niches and pilasters, and addressing the principal paintings. This entire work, known simply as 'The Ceiling' is epic in scale, imagination and treatment, and is set in a painted pudo-architectural white framework of lunettes, severies, spandrels, pilasters—a 'virtual' web of triangular, rectangular and curved forms.

Finally, looming unframed out of the beyond is the ultimate power: 'The Last Judgment' fresco. It depicts Christ's return, saints and martyrs ascending; and sinners descending, or being dragged panic-stricken into flames near a demonic Charon's boat.

It is an embroiled cauldron of some four hundred figures where all is awe, confusion and energy as 'souls' are embodied in the resurrection of the dead.

Notes to the text of the poem are indicated by an asterisk (*) on relevant Movement or verse numbers. These notes are on pages 102-110.

Prologue — The Gaze

(Verses 1-5)

THE SISTINE CHAPEL, ROME, MAY 2009

MOVEMENT 1*   (*Verses 1–5*)

The Gaze

1

As I stand beneath and drink the juices of the sky, she sits
    on the floor, upright, alone, in meditation.
The softening posture of her limbs, her given space,
    her body garlanding solitude's deep silence, host me
through closed eyelids, tell me wait. Her ankles are
    crossed, her knees high, spread under a flowing pale-
    pink dress
to thigh her resting arm and set elbow. The jacket's quiet
    green is comfortably warm. Her left hand touches her
    cheek; thumb and forefinger tell.

2

This face centres a still point, draws me up and in. She is
    waiting. I attend.
A man and child watching from behind her enigmatic
    form seem to toll me.
Overhead a ram's horny skull and bronzed nude men
    turn to watch elsewhere.
What is there here to trade desire for empathy – the
    body's rude survival? its pleasure in the chase?

3*

Nearby, where power bends under its own busy-ness,
    beauty sublimate in young man's limb, torso, mouth,
    buttock, thigh and genitals,
unburdens human stock in tinted sheaths of eloquent skin.
    Raising arm and knee tilts love's call beyond a fall.
O Libya! such beauty's draught is elemental, pagan and
    eternal ... and beauty
is no surprise when blending mind, body, book and gown.

4

The shadows on this sibyl's limbs are shadows of delight
    in the mind's absorption, not in the sorrows of a
    prophet's well-trod soul
laced by tormented conscience and hooded duty. Grace
    and elegance stand these folds in gold and salmon
    pinks of wisdom and nobility.
The tone of a flowing turn of shoulder or of finely platted
    tresses
sets the open eye in violet ribbon, yellow ochre braid and
    red lined robe.

5

This vault will flood itself in streaming colour currents,
    weaving scapes of memory
in crimson-yellow-pink blue-green gray and white strands
    of twirling waves
for eyes to see and skin to feel; all textured contours of
    attachment, binding bodies—
like carpets of blossom—in this momentary swirl where
    we embrace.

Book 1 — Creation

PART 1: CREATION'S HOLD
(Verses 6-64)

MOVEMENT 2   *(Verses 6–12)*

The force that floats through me

6 *

Up here my craned neck seeks solace where none can
    show light.
My fingers tremble on the lip and my arse,
like god's in wayward pre-existing skies,
 bares to mankind a sphincter of expectation.

7

I can hear vertebrae and muscles creak
and feel their pain as I readjust, twist, undo
my glances, strains and wiles beneath that high
risen *weltanschauung*. Hear me.

8

Is this marbled floor and crowded space below
brimming with human thought and dream
where we must be, where we find some cause
and casket, whale and bream, shoal and shawl?

9

I like that face and silent presence. The gaze.
But in this same moment, movement overpowers
a yellow bittern secreting her vaulted story
in the naked architecture of creation's way.

10

Here the earthenware jars break, or pour
nourishingly as limpid penis, fulsome testicle
and questing eyes of many noble *ignudi*
beam glandular worlds with every shoulder's turn.

11

Who you are is not important. What is here
is who you are. Who I am too is not important.
What I am is here, aware, active – though difficult and
cowardly spiraling may cloud my shine, my sheer.

12

Your shine and sheer swan into the mists,
rescuing and losing in one gigantic laugh,
that echoes the peals hidden in your brush.
Chip that mix, mix that powder, paste, splash, cry.

Within the act

13

When light first spilled from the great void,
did it know the motions taut within its rays, waiting
to be spun and spat forth? —waking day
and leaving night behind. Is that divide our time?

14

When the darkness comes again – and we can be
as what and who we are, movement
in a foreign chapel of dis-ease and stress
that teases every particle we cherish – time will cease.

15

But we are now and time inoculates and feeds us.
So maybe look around, re-sensitize the body-brain
to what we call universe – this all in one
which so enthralls, endures, releases and imprisons us.

16

Without its walls and floors, ceiling'd halls and doors
and all the myriad images to distract and teach,
we might each, as some chief wisdom source,
spend energies we steal and borrow to invent.

17

We like to indulge pretence leaning against the fence
to scan horizons for neighbourly determinations,
for potential trials we see as challenges
to prove somehow that we can and will explode the bomb.

18

We know the power is there. We know we can assimilate
and be assimilated in layers of layers-mash
in some chicken house we choose and cherish for ourselves,
as if a feather bed for rutting skies and folding fate.

19

We know the simple things but we strut into deceit;
we bypass the ruffs and folds of thought or intuition,
we journey without ladder, scaffold, crane or desk,
and with pillage, rape and rule we damn discovery.

20

Let's see what we can build — some honest construct
as our hammock between sky and clay, night and day,
bed and board, bark and bole — somewhere the dance
that is, or that is not, becomes a visible and wisdom jig.

21

I do not dance you say? Then, find a floor, some shoes,
a door into the spoor of wave that wallows by, swim
in the embrace of ether, blood and brine; and flitter
in the sunlight to trace a path and trawl the shore.

22

If the flows of torrent, and flare defeat and drain
your energy and hope, relax. The world knows you are
    a feeble thing.
Let the flood be; finger-play its melody to find your song;
    lyric
the open flesh; the tune will step you barefoot through
    its bars.

23

Strong and without fear look back to know;
look down to weigh the way; look ahead to gauge options
your form aspires to space; look up to find *al fresco* mirrors
framed within your eyes: here is where to paint your dreams.

As dark and light disperse

24

Did Adam's apple fall? Or was it Eve? I dreamed I was the tree
plucked and outed as a man, and left to wander in that garden
on my own, abandoned by the lovely pair who mated there
and grafted their own branches. I must bind mine.

25

Or was it my first Eve, sate beneath me,
plucking through time the serpentine harp strings
of my loom, ignoring sun, moon and rubbish dump
till goaded by her sting, the reprimander stang?

26

This body of mine confuses me – and sometimes you.
It shoulders all I need, it reseeded, shaped and struck
a pose for survival schooled on this for'm we hold firm.
We have no other one. Though I might sculpt me better.

27

As a rub of lipstick from your lips on my thumb
will leave a trace of darkness on well smeared skin
releasing any lead within its base, our journeys, mired
on every track we trace, betray, display, or sing dumb.

28

But I like kissing your lips clean, brightly firm and full;
I like tasting your touch and mixing our clay ready for bedding
into autumn's winter, summer's spring, and covering
with hands' harrow and hold, heaving muscle, hair and skin.

29*

My eye wanders to the sky where angels seem to thrive
as messengers discoursing neural currents between then and now
and show the universe in virginal blue, pinpricked with silver's gold.
What has an apple got to do with this? Who gives a fig! Our kiss
  emboldens its golden hue.

30*

So mix the plaster well. The full bucket will space
a day for our creation under Jonah's railing eye
and arching pose as, spread with lioncloth power
and leaning back, he sees a world he scarcely knows unfold.

31

Three days and three nights in a whale's belly
reassure the body of the power that it relies on.
What point angers, shouts and stones? Sit back and think:
then carve the rock you have to carve – and knock twice.

32

I still swim in that whale's belly where life's offals float,
fanciful, profound and bare; drugged by the grandeurs
that hide nakedness in flesh grown soggy, dour.
I exercise each day to find my hour and tend my vine and fin.

33

As a child I followed Jonah into the belly of that whale;
not in argument with hands that gesture nor swallowing bile's
unsavoury glug. It was for adventure, voyage and vision—for action
in the mystery of a belly more than human, not divine

34

but with the power of brimstone and a language of its own
—a great cathedral chapel to explore and know, to sieve the secrets
of its bones and gut to followers of woe, to swop
tears for story's joy underneath this happier outside sky.

I too begin with scaffolding

35*

I too begin with scaffolding. That clumsy undigested mess
of bone without muscle hanging from the ceiling must be gone.
Away with it! That was not my construction.
It gave no thought to my design, nor to my need.

36

Away with it! Take it down and let this noble arch
hold free to breathe and welcome pigmentation's glow.
I make my own steps, stays and pulleys, a bold rib
suspension, holding me and feeding on the elasticity of skin.

37

Balance; swing; fold and fall.
Set, grip, clasp the mallet.
Carriage, castle, motte and water.
Eve is my daughter.
Planet, plough, harrow, seed.
Temper, colour, cut and weave
the conversation basket of a morning
through to hasty supper.

38

Knot, knarl, knurling symptoms,
breasts cut, pentacles cast,
frieze, plaster bubble;
slowly waken barren testicles
to shape and shatter shoal and shipwreck.
Upside down, this hold is full of dream.
We dream, we dry; we drown in torrents
of another's making.

39

Haul it down, throw away
the unbending bow.
Slit a sally, notch a cord to sound
a hymn to a new world's melody.
Sing to the hammer's heavy strokes
and gentler taps. Re-spring dance
on earth's new floor, fit wheels
with open spokes. And strike.

40

Pin-point one star, a well or stone.
It may be the lover won
or leader lost; or manner,
grace and gravity overcome.
Hang here high and happy,
painting pictures in a sky
of wise and stupid men who lace
their time with ignorance.

41

Being is a cautionary tale – of knowledge tuned with honour
and humour – it needs no recognition past itself.
Anyone may listen, may look on brighter days
to share the vault and drink my wine. I will build and paint.

The flowing moon

42

Way over capacity, way over capacity. Too many people
too many thoughts, ideas wrestling for attention, leaping
through my head, pounding my skull and losing focus.
This is the day I will begin, this is the day that I began.

43

Massage the plaster, massage the paint, massage the body,
warm the stone, write the words, be inside:
honing hearing howling — harrow harness hide and hole;
lift the treasure, hoist the load, stop and focus. Paint the day.

44

Forty days and all in vain, forty nights alone. Forty images
to haunt each movement, song and splay. Deluge, danger
dark the day. Night is never near, listen here to the flowing moon
in the hot sweat on every madman's asking brow. To work. Now.

45

My lover's come, abandon ship, jump the rails, down the pole.
She's here, she's here – we're now, we're high – above the ring
of slow burning heat making sweet smelling peat and logs of oak.
This is the bright shadow of sunshine, my bracing day. Our end.

46

There is a moment in preparation or disputation when all
becomes irrelevant or insubstantial; but work remains to do.
In that moment, valleys grow into blossom; and they leave behind,
afar and cold, checkpoints at crossroads. I choose to know.

47*

I make my way like a Blasket island bull,
undeterred by water. All pannus, penis, testicle and dark,
each night is welcoming and welcome for its brighter light.
Here is my vane, my vein rush—needle fill, bottle spill,

48

a bucket mixed and full, a cow's hair brush, a feather quill.
The bull of the north has had his choice — hell's the ugly one —
with scarcely a glance beyond. Lily-proud she draped aloft
the drab shawl to burn her slender elegance on this stall.

In the grip of the uncanny

49

She was there—she always is, invisible and teasing
on summer's day in Rome, in the queue outside the walls;
we waited, talked, looked and smirked, quipped patiently
then sped past baroque hanging halls to raid the Sistine.

50

In the grip of the uncanny we walk without pause or
tempting silence intervene and give us some measure of hold.
Do not wait, my friend, her stride implied, silence has no
   need of you.
Have me while you may, and surpass the wilderness.

51

I could jump now; dive perhaps, a clean break and graceful
departure from this artifice, the heavens and imagination.
Who would care beyond that first emotional tearing of the fabric,
the spattered blood and marbled visibility of jagged fleshy bone.

52

We wandered through the gaming halls, you and I among the makers
of the moment, searching for conversation. Enticements to spin
wheels hover on our heels like silent snapping mutts impatient
with the slow turning. Holding hands and looking at your lips

53

I leaped and flew us limbs akimbo through the emptiness,
wildly laughing at the rush of blood and air in the space
we colour on the wind to cross the void. Do angels happen here?
In flight, afloat; in fall; in spin; in love; lusty on this wonder-loft.

54

Out of control, our bodies take the heat and lead.
Calling voices drive our spinning song in this heady bowl
we neither knew nor wanted to, beyond the thrust
and expectation of our dancing tangle limbs.

55

The melody was indeterminate, and wrong; the rhythm false,
the patterns overdone. A hidden war engendering the swan
and Leda – gently suckle, man and woman; we want to change
into new forms to spin globes and seize the pole's uncertain grip.

56

Behind us the toil of our enthusiasm is joy
infiltrating ether's pall to evaporate and reshape ghosts
that freely flow beyond the world we are. Our seed
absorbed and sown will live on. Now, back to work!

* * *

57

Why turn down my invitation? It aches still within. The tone
dismissive, the words clear. How can you know my touch
without visiting my bed, sharing my house, browsing my library,
sitting at my table, talking, resting, sexing on my battered couch?

58

Disrobed, couched and crouching parted thighs
in temperas semblance, softly muscled, womanly
in wait, delicate of face, mouth, nose and piercing eyes.
My long neck, my beak, my wings arouse, emboss,

59

undress desire; and tender quill, vane and fin.
Within your petal form, intoxicate, indulgent, softening
to absorb and drink the moistening brine, and breathing deeply
we awaken physic, and rise ingesting apple acid at our heaven's gate.

We lie in wait

60

Here between this scaffold floor and ceiling we wait
the sharing of a second vision; but as morning drifts
the vigours of the day bring other plans; we go to work,
you swiftly on those wings of gossamer and goose, me in my boots.

61

When you are gone, a shadow slows my way,
envelops me in gloom and irritation at
the vastness of the vault, the space to fill with colour.
Thought curdles over rapids to a sullen turning pool.

62

Getting lost is not a condition men like me endure or venture
    on today.
All GPS and mobile interlinks enmesh our every step or slip
    without mercy.
The mood and mode of language slips too, and abandons silence
to the noise of angry, rash and insignificant collision.

63

Perhaps it is time to begin without the beginnings we have been,
to journey without the maps we made or borrowed from those
    unknown travellers
who, indifferent to the scapes and soils they journeyed on,
were themselves scoped, scraped and scattered without care
    or thought.

64

Let's go. Let's go. I have the whereabouts to win a smile
for any traveller with the balls to fly, the breasts to show,
with feet unfettered and ready to run. Up on this wall,
    up on this floor, high up above
on the curved and arching sky, and through the in-between.
Let's go. Let's go!

Book I — Creation

MOVEMENT 9   *(Verses 65–67)*

Convinced we are awake

65

> *Enmasse.*
> Like a myriad mollyblooms and blooms
> in some spectral wormry
> oiled and warmed up, lugubriously
> writhing in and through and over under
> anywhere there is to go
> in this wundersensuous and idle soppy sexing
> of the populace. This long before
> eve'nadam's game came to grief's gruff and puff.

66

Enmasse. Bearing all the heavy weight of gravity on bone
    and hair and flesh
no matter how arisen or engorged with all that blood of
    passion's pain and prettiness.
Or all the coming and the going and the return again.
        Squirm, brim, broth, brew;
        loosen, stretch, streamline, strew.
    Like an earthworm crawl a slither through.

67

Our bodies all re-mass in this cosmo-mess of particles speed-oozed
from the out in of the big bang's bong. Ding dong, ding dong,
    dong ding.
What do we do to know except continue as we are and stay
    the stay until the rain
stops or the clouds break. Like ruminating cows in gondolas,
    we're passing through convinced we are awake.

The cartoon will draw itself

68

When summons come we read the signs.
We make a list—a clamouring in colour,
to swallow, digest, vomit, excrete—to tell
before time fixes and discards us.
The work remains to follow or abandon.
I no longer care, for it is there—
there for crossing of our Styxes
and for filling Charon's boat.

69

When I complain 'tis for the honour
in great art. Indulge me—
my platform has its needs:

70*

Master masons and *garzini* to prepare
the ground (above me and below).
I need men to do my bidding,
who will not shame my fresco
— painters good at fictive relief,
cornices, tondi, and thrones,
at drafting storylines for my cartoons.
Twenty ducats per month for each.
Someday all will have to go for I am
my own prophet and sibyl
and though hard pressed and out of sorts
I need no friends to make my work:

71

      — just one to come and go,
    to tell my days and with my trust
       — that's Giovanni;
  and a paymaster who will source
my pigments when the scaffolding begins
       — that's Granacci;
    some good men of true fresco
to learn from — that's Bugiardini;
another for his lime, tufa, pozzolana,
    and engineering wonderments
       — my Bastiano;
   a man to scrape and plaster all
and do whatever else is necessary
    — Piero di Jacopo Rosselli;
and also Indaco: di Pietro Torni
   — a man that I can send for figs.

72

    I need reams of paper
      for cartoons
    — a myriad to do
    for I will intervene
    to show my hand.
  Delphi's throne is mine,
and the better for it too.
   A *giornate* schedule
  — each day's paint will soak
     the deluge.
  —— we must destroy, renew,
  revisit and explore even
if doubt is the loss of six days' work
    and fear of more.
The artist ferries on his shoulder,
  living or dead, his *pentimenti*.

73*

'I need a certain amount of pretty blues
for I have ... things to paint here.'
Egyptian blue for god's dominion,
the waters of oceans, and the Flood.
Azurite, and lapis lazuli mined
at great expense beyond the Sinai.
Some ground coarse for pigments
that are richly dark,
some very fine
for pale ethereal skies and seas
pale before our dawn,
or for garments' folding flows
in blues, yellows, pinks and greens.
Light for the fire of gods,
for turban, hose, blanket weft and weave,
and for the shadows of life-giving night.

74

Such colours hewn and mixed
with mortar and pestle become
instruments of form and understanding,
gracing the eye and pouring majesty
onto the priests and penitents below,
craning necks and postures to route
the gradient of brilliance that oozes
through in saturated hue and tone,
with *cangiante*—colour change
for rise and fall,
rotund muscle or body turn,
for lift and wrap
and textured shadow in the fabrics
and the skin, the hair and fingers,
toes or downcast eye, noses,
arms and thighs.

75*

I had my scaffold made to hold court and paint.
I don't need to cover my nakedness,
this platform is my ark. I mock myself, and well.
Twenty naked men will hold the world
together, garland nature, challenge god
— Savonarola's voice will surely thunder
at such honesty and question beauty's dangers.
Seven bible prophets; five pagan Sibyls,
hosts of gentle *putti* voices, pudgy children
to conform, converse, and sign
to tell as any boy or girl will.
Two executions in defence of tribe;
a brazen serpent, curative on Tau,
and an orphan 'fair and beautiful'
(— who now will rescue Mordecai?
who will be his Haman, crucified, not hanged?)

76

And all around fine people streaming
stories from the household floor.
In all their colours: skin, light brown,
pinks and whites; yellow hair, and auburn,
dark and light greys; and eyes
dark or distant, brown, cold, startled,
eager, or closed in meditation, prayer or fear.
The elegance of cheek and chin,
the power of a well-made nose,
fingers busy, toes a-splay;
firm and muscled arms,
woman or man, seed and flower.
Families of searching faces, wondrous looks,
calling lip and stern eye; Magdalens
and Marys wearing colour's warmth;
limpid, deep and strong.

77

And colours' loves between the folds
and cloaks of service to their pending dreams:
with ochre braids, yellow bands,
full-bodied folding reds and pinks
and greens, in pale or bright
or deepened hue to dress a tale.
Buckles, clasps of gold, shawls
and scarves of mitred whites
and sleeves woven light
and brightly wound around.
Pregnant women, tall women,
working women, fighting women,
sexy women bedding men,
and my woman, deep in meditation;
all strong child-bearing creatures
their bodies tall in poise and past.

78

Elegant men at work,
men reading, idling, men ennobled
by their cloaks of gold, green and blue;
men with hard chiselled features
and hawk-like beaks;
and soldiers.
Among the race of men and women
bound for final places in eternity,
those unwilling to resolve their nature
for itself and find satisfaction within.
It must be god or paradise or the viscous
fires of a hell they've stoked so well.
We die of body and in soul,
yet feed on poisonsuckle
supped with relish
from the flame of power.

79

If it chooses to observe and learn,
the eye will see a world
of brazen flames that spiral
toss and turn to change and burn
to tease and toll and spell
a people's story here on my ceiling.

80

Watch my colours bed the day and night
with fresh dawns of truth and joy
to slake the painful belly of despair
The stony white flesh of my *Ignudi*
is soft to tease harmonious light
into a pleasure bouquet
for my celestial palette
of body dressed
and styled
as story.
Mosaic pavements curve
varieties of yellow, green and brown
to trail my architecture, sourcing
robes, cloaks and underwear
of yellow-ochre, pale-yellow or apple-green
in gradients reaching yellow-grey and yellow-brown

81

then sliding back to acid apple
or a dress of pure and simple green.
Red slopes its lay to pink
or violet dissolution, stitched
with threads of violet grey.
Or journeys all the way from blue
to greenish ochre orange;
or, travelling by vermillion cinnabar, in white,
dove-gray and rose-red through all the blues.

Skeins of fully saturated hues and colour change
will tone, highlight, shadow, model and dilute.
White variations will seed to apple-green
or plum rotundity with shadow on a thigh,
revelling in fabric's echo of its time, taste
and iridescent truth. Variety is my clarity,
purity my colour power.

82*

As with marble I do not need
a steady drum. My mallet
tests the grain, my eyes listen
for the pulse of stone my picks
release. This fresco lark is not
an art for an old man's bone

Beneath the hard breath of a curious god

83

Alone at last and ready to begin the work of mediation.
　　Pour the plaster dust and pour the water.
Crush the pigment with mortar and pestle, round the
　　rhythm, round and round
until the colour merges with your eyes, excites your
　　brain. And more. Then climb
into the clouds and hide away. Nobody cares, somebody
　　pays. Keep me in your mind as I play.

84*

The first day, I made the world out of the clay that I was
　　given. Doing it my way may not have been so wise.
The end is my beginning but my beginning is my end in
　　the circle of the sun.
My grave was made before I came, and I've been
　　searching for another grave
not measured in the nave of any great or small cathedral,
　　or tomb with forty marble effigies.

85

My dreams were often slithery and wet with nut-brown
　　hair and catechisms.
Now you are here, eye to eye with my cast wrinkled nape
　　and horizontal brow.
Here, a dribble on your nose is an accident I can redo;
　　you look like my friend but you are not he.
In centuries to come who will you be? Time continues
　　to pretend.

86

Back to work. The mind does its own and needs to let my
  hands do this cursed painting.
One portion of a half of one day done. How many hopes
  to go? I will complete it before you are dead. You will
  see and still be blind.
There is no blind man on my ceiling — all below is
  visible and docked.
The purse is full, the larder swollen by the flood; the
  souls all dull stock.

87

I have lost my way as sky and planets separate beneath the
  hard breath
of a curious god, whirl winding through an unmade cosmos.
Up here I have become invisible, just to myself perhaps.
  That daub recognises me – I can tell.
Stings and stigmata hold no grip atop the canopy of work.

88

It doesn't take long to understand that there are no popes
  or kings. But down there
are young things, hi-kicking legs about their necks,
  knickerless betimes,
who burrow underneath the throbbing of a thousand
  penises to reason ways out.
Who's for kings or cardinals when young men fail.
  Between youth and age so much is contradictory.

Such beauty and its solitude are radical

89

She. I would like to paint her. Give her this place. Show
    her gentleness to this harsh creation.
Give hope to some pilgrim searching my cabinet for
    direction and new ritual. Hunkered on this spandrel
in seated ease, with pink and soft-green folds across her
    covered knees and breasts, and neatly braided hair,
her presence flows to the floor below. Such beauty and its
    solitude are radical.

90*

O Giovani, pray for my cramps and spasms and
    headaches; I'm getting goitre from the strain,
my belly suckling on my chin and colours from my brush
    distain the ceiling, flush my face,
my buttocks taut and tense in unprotected flight, as we
    create our vegetation up above.
My skin is stretched, starched and knotted in judgement:
    rescue me from this place, release the Syrian bow.

91

Let's go. To the heart of it for otherwise there will be no
    heart in it,
only narrative and unworthy information distracting time
    or space.
Here is a new place, here in this sky. Here where I can lie
so truth will out and seal itself, spun into the sinews and
    the ligatures of light.

***

92

At noon bells strike across the city, a caul of prayer. Some
    pass untouched,
some sing, some bow their heads and pause. Man is a
    silent thing afloat
on air in elemental waves. That god is dead now has no echo.
Listen to the thunder of strings on oak, housing the
    note's decay.

93

When music hoists between its beat and bend, ways to
    list and flow,
to rise and slide, to fall then climb high again into the
    clouds of theory
we pursue and track through all our journeys, none is so
    urgent as the dreamscape
we protect at night and then betray unwittingly. Will
    scorpio strike pisces' call?

94

Those stars are gone that shaped that sky. I repaint their
    radiance in flesh—and who am I?
Watch me carefully. Beneath my brush and hammer
    there's more than meets your eye.
Eight months in a quarry muscling stone hardens a man,
tests sinew, eye and patience. It penetrates the muscle-bone.

95

Here comes the light, bright and dim; praise him in haste
    across the skies
he makes while I stand with my back arched, straight
    from the belly
of some deep shark not yet created. I sprawl like a
    drunken querulous schoolmaster
gazing, staring, arguing, learning, nakedly observing why.

96

Here too are moons and suns aplenty, and planet earth in
    lone bloom
of root, leaf, and seeding things, forest densities and fruit.
The heat and cold, the fast and slow, rise and fall, the
    hard clay and soft air
all feed Adam's ape, colour, skin and muscle, finger-
    claiming life

97

with languid, limpid, coming eye and lie: on this rock,
    not of it.
He is a form I like to love, and as the plaster dries and
    tints the textures
I have tasted in my mouth and on my fingers like juices
    from my body, these pigments
give life, and with it a desire to smile into creation's craw.

98

God speeds fast to claim his *giornata* and, without
    revelation or my intervention,
unsheathes a shell where mystery huddles underneath its
    billowing spell
a Venus Aphrodite Cleopatra—a Medbh Morrigan
    Magdalen—all Mary on the eve
of this day's space. My Eve, my nursemaid, mother,
    martyr, mirror me.

99

Tell me why. Tell me why in this now almost earth you sit on,
very happily and true in composition and intent, must
    you test your presence?
Why not, your body shouts. And mine. This world we
    make together out-gods our gods for all their wisdoms
    and deceits.
We are where we perceive. Why, then, an inquisition,
    a question? This leaf?

100

From hand to hand, to hold and set within and seal the
    answers—is that sin?
Is what you are and I, together or apart, eyes open to this
    art, the mirror of creation's dust,
the knowledge in our heads, just light's reflections we
    career in?
We dress and deck the body physical. We pose and lust.

Why I find it in my mind to paint

101*

The body beautiful is diminished to our cost. Out, out!
    the serpent cries. Bent and bowed
with aged harrowed skin we leave the paradise we belong
    to for another. We wonder
that the power within us held then lost the power
    beyond, that fruit and plough become
labour and love to host the slaughters we have blossomed
    towards and built upon.

102

Paradise engendered here is possible — that's why I find
    it in my mind to paint.
Now that the apple's plucked, the fig eaten and man and
    woman pillared to pillage the world's potentials,
the sword that points the way is double-edged. My
    fingers hold the oak and acorn to the kill
and the living figtree binds man and serpent as they rise
    to Eve.

103

She will turn to taste the juices of the clay, breast the
    tumescent figs of life,
and sprout below my canopy to spring anew, to rut, to
    ultimately trust the universe.
Opening to the seasons' flow, she will not blush through
    procreation.
My arches, painted to release the ageing pair, and to revive
    the stem, will test the shedding of the serpent's skin.

104

In lust's heave is there power to trust indifferent desire?
    Man or woman
made of clay and heat betray the knowledge they possess,
    and may not awake
until the big bang returns its measurements for science
    and maths to calculate and poet painters to re-sculpt.
Do tenderness and lust score music for a universe more
    ducted to an earth that is not paradise?

* * *

105*

Noah understood the law. He made his ark to float above
    human detritus and shallow skies.
In this cadaverous enclave, I too float on fallow fees at
    liberty to be. What I choose to do makes me.
I may reconstruct this thing we are as Noah built on
    water the world he was, thinking in pairs to rut
and not to rue a universe abandoned. To be is what we
    are; to do avers to be.

106

In its slough creation's underbelly, skin and rough terrain
    await the dove's descent for leafy proof
of restoration. Warts and all. Stuff is hard to slay or
    swallow amid slime of pit and pool
like all first thoughts and strange ideas. Move on. Move
    on; give man a place with tools to tap
the mould, inspire the rapid burst of garlic taste and
    smell. Recourse through hell releases sap.

107

Beyond Noah's ark and garden, beyond his drunkenness
    and sacrifice, the sons of man divide
in their haste to serve or suit. We should mount more
    men on crucifixes.

Enough of dead sheep and goats! Blood is spilt on stone
    to prise approval of desire.
The garden spade will turn clay and waste none.

108

None is waste, the worm and dirt, the dung, the
    devastations wrought by dynasty.
For kings and queens all spy the roots and calluses of
    harvest fruits.
It's how rulers rule and kings are made. Blood thickens later.
In deluge currents, cascades of seed, flower, leaf and
    branch race beneath harrow and plough.

* * *

109

I am the voice of angel too, the arrow speeding through
    hopeless air to rise you from your chair
with swift clean strike through bone and flesh; love darts
    through soft tissue silently.
There is this story to tell of intrusion on time's private
    spaces as creation beats like a searching heart
for blooded rhythms of meaning and for action it can
    rhyme with art.

110

With a core of all the words spoken since time on earth
    began,
bypass the blood of mothers and fathers' pride; abandon
    siblings to their destinies – not ours to trace.
With knowledge harvested in stone or thrown as
    pigmentation on walls and ceilings,
unveil this landscape's effervescing revelation in the
    shadows that we cast as sin.

111

As with sky and sea in mirror view stalling the tide and
    wind, waves billow to a ghost horizon
low above my head, and clouds, afloat beneath, soften the
    water's thunderous undertow.
There are spaces to infill. Between the shadow and the
    clarity of dreams
that wait awaking, we sow doubt, and string dark
    reflections everywhere.

112

Sin is an atrophy we hesitate to own, though we reek
    ambivalence and doubt
on what is good or not in what it is we fail to be. From
    what bed does night look askance
at the magnificent to scale its crucifixion and stigmata
    when
    all we need
are words of admiration drafted with compassion for the
    flesh and bone we are?

The centrifuge—forms I can release

113

The rough stone block will survive me. Though lovely to
   my eye, unless I release its Ka to sun, wind and rain,
the block will remain unknown. To pick and point its flesh,
   I must insert myself.
The forms I can release from cold stone are the purpose
   of my hand and eye.
A final polish to cheek or thigh, to open lip or swell of
   muscle limb, is for the dark and light.

114

The shadows in this vault excite me. I can fill and brush
   its heavens with gods and angels,
wonder tales, heroes, heroines and dreamers, from creation
   to the judgement of resurrected man.
I can restore imagination, spill its floods and flourishes,
   its prophets and sibyls,
its *putti* and *ignudi*, its battles, beheadings and sacrifices
   with the making of bread above old Julius' head.

115

And more.
This is a hold for destiny,
storied by brush or mallet
to manifest beginnings
as philosophers and poets might with words.
My colour-change can tell the folds of time
in cloak and hose; my spandrels and lunettes
flood the sky with history's forgotten spate;
here is the telemon for time itself,
the vault's anchor and God's acrobat,
dressing his great mosaic,
polishing the belly and buttocks of fate.

116*

A blessing and a curse are what I need to ride this horse.
I must dismount to be the man I am.
For whose feet fit my lame gait? Whose strong mind has
set us free, this poet here and me?
Pale or bright, thought framed to paint a ceiling, arks a
route to heaven's gate.
We sail apart, we await sunbeams to heal our dreams —
and all the better if we've fought and tested fate.

END OF BOOK 1

Book 2 — Eternal Day — The Work

(Verses 117-205)

MOVEMENT 15 *(Verses 117–121)*

The elemental waits inside

117

When I stand here, raise my arms, and breathe the air
    with all its floating things,
particles, dustmites, atoms, nuclei, waves invisible or
    audible, and undiscovered elements
whose cavities are yet to find, I absorb their purposes
    deep in my chest and belly
to create images to re-stress this ceiling's silent vault;
    and lay in it all my life and then more.

118

The plaster's here, the scaffolding in place, my painter
    friends still gambol with my love.
The pigments mixed and tested, cartoons in hand,
    powder bags to pounce, trace or scatter black dust
    to the margins,
knives to incise new decisions. To begin at the beginning
    is never possible for brush or mallet. This is a question
    every picture asks
but finds answer in completion or abandonment. The
    elemental waits inside the brain; flesh and body will call.

119

I stand outside but not beyond, and not blind. The spade
    that digs this soil digs well and wall;
the strength of arm, thigh and heel, the bow of head and
    eager eye satisfy the body; the seed will grow.
All about, landscape is burnished with fruits of labour,
    figs of love, hurts of accident and lust, spice of
    laughter, spurt of pain.
All are as here as I am now and you who enter will be.
    Garden gates open for those who gather round and dig.

120

So why in this blossoming fall am I about to kill the beast
    and sell its soul to the nether world's control?
I know the metaphor and shade, the after-wards, yet, just
    in case, and for the cycle of creation, I will unharness tales
that resurrect the broken mysteries of a great trek across
    time's pale globe.
Then it can measure me and send another flood to
    vanquish thought. Simplicity itself may once again return.

121

The ground I have to work on is a warp in space, an open
    sky set within its own apocalypse.
Here I conduct *opera dei* for my own satisfaction, and
    without anger eclipse the past, its present and future.
I am a man who sings a song, who knows a lyric, flaunts
    a melody and will not be unheard nor drowned.
    I leap across
the orchestral terraces of Torah, Kabala and Rome. What
    nesting lairs for beauty's host?

Beyond beast and breast

122

How near the gates of heaven are
to the open portals of our hell.
We dream on, careless in meadow,
sifting shades of day to feed
night's untested history,
philosophy's intention, dawn's romance:
morning's expectation.
Why not? Few make time for possibility.
'Tis easier move on than wait first voices to emerge.
We weave and web our headless anonymity with desperate
subterfuge.

123

It's Plato's call, Cuchulainn's ball, Satan's gall
and, up here, this market stall.
All made to nurture purity, holiness, power and time,
images strung high and sprung in every leap.
Better far to mock and make a joke, for few will die of
laughter,
or when foreshortened vie undressed.
These pictures, paintbrushes and pigments,
though colouring a likely story, exist beyond beast and breast.

Lovers of the earth

124

When a heavy summer fog pours through suburban limbs
    chilling and fouling
in soupy nothingness neighbouring eyes, arms, legs and
    bodies,
and like some lurking indeterminate beast its terrorising
    intimacy
is heavy, silent and slow, what dimensions, depths,
    expanses can there be?

125

—Or when in moderate latitudes, an unforeseen white
    cumulous pillars up the sky
to dominate, and hover through the day dressing its
    produce for the sump of blackness down below
and walking on hills for exercise or contemplation, we
    find snows begin to lull
the earth to sleep isolating thought within the swirl and
    flurry of a cold persistence

126

—so does the god wake itself on this ceiling, a soaring
    sombre unembroidered impulse of design
determining things possible under a sky-blue billowed shell.
And it becomes—the first day and the last as light is
    wrenched apart from dark, muscle-mauled
from nothingness to its opposing pole, flexing shadows
    that lurk in twilight curls.

127

This world is now become.
                Stand back and watch.
                    Climb down
            and be the first to sour the origins we seek

behind the big bang:
a face in turmoil staring left and right, up and down:
                        this is a broad-brush day's cloak
in bellowing browns and pinkish hues; joy and boldness
        everywhere,
                        in and out of time.
Boldness needs no rest and in an instant, powerful arms extend
        and cup the distant marshes
                        of creation's nether lip.

128

Skies we recognise begin to pounce the *intonaco's* visibility,
and starbursts rush to fill eternity's expanding maw. Moon
and sun transpire in a headrush from nothingness to scene.
Things of awe, bating breath, scatter water, dry the land,
plant the ground and seed seas with creatures great and
small. Enough to satisfy the artist of the skies.

129

As pillars of the world,
filled with Atlas
strength, the grace
of Adonis, and the
nobility of man's pleasure
and imagining, a score
of *ignudi* sing, bare in
every pose, in crouch
of shoulder, tilt of thigh,
turn of hand, melodious
offerings of hope, swaying
our canopy with story and potential.

130

We are lovers of the earth, not its spouses bound or
bought. We are siblings of the stars, sating history's well.
Lovers live in beauty's orbit, bypassing time. We change
words to love all over again; we mould our shadows with
pigments; we make alternatives.

131

I do so here – gyrating for this ceiling, spinning my
  history and damning it
with ocean's praise and Sinbad's song for Jesus. Hunger in
  the desert
turns a poet's thought to flesh, to tourist breakfasts,
  dancing dinners, tea
and the sweet desserts of irony invisible to chalk, cheese
  or soap.

132

We grasp and grope for baubles to embellish reputation,
  to fill bulging pockets,
to feed and foul the intellect, the body's clasp. Soul
  journey is a locket
dangling midstream well-fed breasts and numbed nipple rash.
  Undressed,
man and woman are poet painters who will grace a dance,
  invent, devise.

133

See how these fingers reach to touch the other worlds
  we share.
Observe the languorous lilt of expectation;
like an udder woven with the tougher sinews of eternity,
it is an invitation to embrace softer gentility.

134

Light and beauty swing on un-distracted bars of rhythm,
feeding colour, rhyming story, strumming melancholy
in bursts of healing melody as we are drawn like Eve,
  open to our fate
—tomorrow is the what, the where, the who we are.

Excitements of transience

135*

I am a sickle up here, my neck twisted with pain,
my back a gardener's agony, my eyes slow to tell –
but, friend or enemy, poet, teacher, prostitute, this is
    a kitchen
stocked to bake bread, to make soup, stirring thought
    and the residue of history.

136

Here is my centrepiece and body beautiful
vesting light and dark in a drunken spiralling of
    desperation and display.
Every thought is built of meadow green or mountain blue.
Through open skies
our eyes reach for the contours of wisdom.

137

Once, a story told of man's dominion over fish in the sea,
    fowl in the air,
cattle on land, every creeping thing. Dues imagined in
    creation's premise.
But creatures of such beauty may subvert the teller's art,
    so story found a narrative,
configured as verb will find its noun, to predicate and
    subjugate landscape's tension and potential.

138

This AdamEve we are comes sweetly forth with suppliant
    palms as if acknowledging
at times the God, at times the self. Where is the need of
    purple robe and stern authority

to take us to our beds, and make another? ... make another?
... make another? ... Make a mother.
Life is what we live. Death means life. Flesh our death.
Thought disrobes our knowledge. Desire?
A parrotfish at sea.

* * *

139

This is my work up here, and down below. We sleep; we
then awake to sleep again
fulfilled by acquisition of knowledge, the ova and the
sperm of our creation.
Is body a foundation or a dressing beautiful, replete with
the hope of elementary truth?
The flesh I paint excites my brain, the hue and form of
every shadow undo me and release me.

140*

Darkness in sleeping and waking is my *terribilità*:
the pleasure it unleashes and imprisons: the snog and shag
of lip and breast;
the sweat and groan; the groin; the foaming spoil; the
pouring forth
of semen as salmon for our dreams; and the turning on
to light.

141

Image spells my dream
and speeds my brush and chalk;
it is the swelter of imagination.
Love is a paint brush spreading hush
and lover's breath on my chest.
Fear precedes and follows the crusading mind,
impressing half-torn tales with history.
The shorn body in its unrecorded grave
has no thought nor time
for beauty to become.

142

Imprisoned in the convulsed excitement of this transient
trapeze,
shackled to imponderability and sway, and with lips to kiss,
we wander through the carnival, losing sight of camels in
the high grass.
Like acrobats carousing on stardust floors—the fire of
death is what we live on.

I have my own work to do

143

Let me to work, friend. Mercury and Venus are in the
house of Jupiter.
I am Michelangelo Buonarroti – Michelagnolo – maker of
marble souls.
But you, hanging with me in this hallowed vault where
God himself may bide,
who are you to sing songs, to cry yes, or no? Virtue pigs
for its own acorns, grows its own oak. Be off!

144

I have my own work to do. The one who's able never fails
to climb this stairs. Today
a final touch will seal this *giornata*, satisfy the boar and
let me on.
The weight of hoar fills cloaks of green, folding mountain
crusts and dipping waves.
Where to begin? —with Zechariah's tale of kings on
donkeys, seeking what we cannot find under leaves of oak.

145

We are no longer young. Our tales abound with giants
brought to ground
and great men losing heads in search of power, bedding
with their executioners, and drunk to boot.
From such fated narrative and coloured plaster man may
find a route; for inside every madness we indulge
in abstract or material form, in plain or woven cloth, are
voices in the wings, opening mountain passes.

146

The folly flapping at our skin needs deeper sutures and
   stitches to hold when bouncing
on the gravity of suns and stars we barely know. Jacob
   foresaw and Joseph too: ready for hard times,
willing to spell the glancing rhymes in Delphi's crystal
   eye, asserting ambiguity, and holy Joel's promises
of corn, wine and oil in abundance, as tribes debate fore-
   knowledge in words written on his scroll.

147

How do we tackle life? As we bridle our horses and race
   them without saddles on sand; or with harness and
   collar push
to plough our meadows and hope to sow for harvesting?
   Better plant apples and figs — there's more fun in
   plucking
to taste the sweetness, and in sunning the skin — or
   entwining vine with limbs that limber up grapes and
   fresh wine.
The simpleton trusts the past to foretell, riding side-saddle
   on reality. The hammer, mallet, paintbrush and pen

148*

blood our stones, our trees, our lambent words; they
   extract honey from the dark and fire from sparks that
   pass at night.
I find light in this vault ere the sun rises. And light in my
   mind when I hear prophet and sibyl.
Now this brightness must be sealed, here, and in marble, for
   there's poison in smoky dialogue and gunpowder
   rhythms.
Each is his own defensive architect and bridge builder.
   We make for ourselves the scaffolding we think
   worthy of our weight.

149*

The north wind blows in winter months indifferent to my
    mortar's mix of lime and pozzolana from the bowels
    of earth.
This damned plaster won't dry in the wind and mocks
    with its spotty mould, flaking skin and pigmentation.
Sangallo and my Pope say carry on, explain the
    weathering and damp and swear that patience and
    gentle scrubbing will repair.
Artifice may outwit nature, hide its ugliness? My head
    grows soggy in despair.

I had this dream

150*

I had this dream. I had this dream that I would carve a well of
    bodies hacked from marble, write a poem in stone
to lift my mind; but lines on paper for this fresco lift my soul.
    I did not know that eight months in the quarries at Carrara
would toll choice slabs now waiting on the shore, and more
    here accusing me.
Yet, I admit the ceiling I despised, the fresco relearned,
    my great migrating Moses, are all in focus now, and
    passionate.

151

I have no idea where this chaos ends. Nor does anyone I
    know, friend, enemy, or pope.
I can measure in *braccio* and coin, in brush or mallet,
    hammer, stone, beauty or betrayal.
The sin I share is genius, aware and ready to exploit the
    body we make truth with,
that body we grow, nourish, test, destroy in columns of
    antiquity or war.

152

What is a completion? — where every page renews, invites,
    reveals; and every morsel knows its own greatness, is
    silent,
patient, attentive; is aswim in store and quarry to pursue
    divergence or to flow passion through....?
Who knows why or how? Who reasons choice for love
    when there is the comfort of certainty and a tendency
to lean against the words of the prophet for answers that
    barter fortune.

153

Give the world to fresco.
Fill the vats with plaster,
    pour the wine.
On trowelling days
open windows, open doors;
    watch burst and bristle
    of colour shape.
Story until each tale is spun.
Though guns and swords may stall a moment,
crack a wall, hold a road, as in the hills and valleys
where trees cascade their leaves for autumn's falling,
the earth in lotus bloom expresses liquid words and sounds.

154

Underneath the Roman soil, in caverns measured by
    gatherings of men who parried god with Caesar,
the young boy who descended into hell found visions on
    its walls, monsters, lovers in free-flowing fantasia,
dragons writhing beneath the god who came to save and
    judge. Images I knew to be
true to the body we host in glory, sacrifice in mind, burn at
    stakes and drown at sea to satisfy revisions we might spin.

155

My scaffolding is barricade and platform in the skies I feign
    and paint
as god made Adam in some ecstatic sperm-burst, languid,
    lonesome man and boy.
It is from where I leach the fiery core to find my genesis
    in art, my pride
in the long drill of Buonarroti, sown and tilled by minds
    that made me.

156

From the centre movement powers forth, sourcing to its
    purpose every bone,
muscle, nerve and ligament beneath skin and bristle, and in
    its living loves and kills.
Its raging diminution becomes night we cannot know before
    we go to sing.
Up here — if art cannot reveal, then neither will mind or
    science alone. Revelation spells and spills our prophecy.

157

As the plaster's mixed and the damp air fills nostrils with
    the lore of pigments on the cusp,
we get drunk on the musty sharpness of lime that galls
    our lungs and dusts the floor.
Our eyes moisten in the slow sear and grit of morning air
    we wait to settle.
Our fingers smudge the thawing rungs to climb each day
    together,
each *giornata*'s populace, my Eve and me. And we know why.

158

This tale ripens as light and dark withdraw to their respective
    corners of the stall
and leave mid-floor uncertainty, distortion and determination,
    tousled as some child's curly hair might be
into a mesh of being and nothingness where self, I and other
    sit like mini-gods awaiting coronation.
The palms of the universe open in invitation to participate,
    to share, to recognise, or to leave be.

159

But a veil draws back, soaking silence from the effigy like
   heat dries off
a clingy morning mist, revealing shadow, obstacle and tracks
   to follow.
The silence melts into a hiss as a distant drone invades
   the space
weaving its thatch everywhere, revelling in dissonance—
   as if tuning for our ears.

160

This hum quivers in the cold dawn, vibrates in rhythmic
   to and fro
like some old man dreading the call to go, unable to decide.
And so the voice of silence lurks, colonised, abstracted,
   diffident, before this onslaught
of a word that has begun to shape itself in hum, drum and
   wave of sound.

161

Underneath that steady rhythm, unforetold,
unexpectedly, a patterning of noises forms
as when a beater sits amidship testing skin and fold with
   unknown intent,
for as yet nothingness must determine its own 'ness' of
   being in the soupy other
of this newborn. There was light, dark and silence—now
   there is sound.

Until we discover the next word

162*

So, here's the clay we know. Word is made a flesh that we
 can bear until we make the next word, and the next
 and then the next again.
Where is our end? How comfortable not to know?
 Bacchus was well made. There is no You that I can see.
Though I break my bones and ache to sculpt, why do I
 return?
Is being here together all; is this my mind? And if I look away,
 where have you gone?

163*

I climbed down the shafts of Rome to view grotesquery
 on walls, and put my hand on it.
Here was a missing piece, a golden house, colour to bring
 above ground, to resurrect,
to paint on ceilings and on new walls. A wakening to be
 carved as Laocoön was made
and floated to the skies before water drowns us and
 returns us to the soil.

164

Enough. Enough. Bring plaster, pigment, brush and trowel.
 The circle turns. We are segments, spokes and sphere.
This yellow here is too dull. Add blues to where the Sibyl
 is and prophet.
Noah's drunk. See him belly on the ground, naked,
 hanging loose and grinning at his punctured sons,
indifferent to their own swinging songs. The times are
 always curious for the living. Go, sacrifice a goat.

The matter is temptation

165

The matter is temptation. Face it, kiss it, paint it.
  My great Eve is Adam, Adam is his Eve. Together,
  birthed of the god
and of the man of god, they fresco here to celebrate their
  sex and generation, lip to hip, eyeing figs and folds
and nesting heaven's generosity. Together sated, fed and
  suckled into muscle, bone and blood, they leave the
  cowl of paradise
and in the body's flame face questions that their
  intercourse has torched. Together in that nest of
  wisdom, bodies

166

seized and sized, not knowing who the lover is will dance
  a bodyglow of comings.
Their walking out—a wildness bleeding satisfaction.
  My Eve. She is beautiful. My Adam too. My garden is
  for me to till.
I trust these hands to make and break, to brush and
  colour, to write a verse.
I live in the smell of our decay, in the amber of caress,
  of plaster touch.

***

167

An angel at the gate saw off shadows of death beneath the
  flame of his sword. The living remain
in their garden, tasting fruit with the serpent, the fruit of
  their bodies, no shame in my lips, no shame between hips,
no shame in this planet twining its serpents and trees, its
  man and its woman,
for these are fruit of its loins, sperm and egg, water and fire,
  clay and air created and garlanded green.

168

The woman said to the serpent, eat of the fruit of the
    garden's trees; and god said,
of the fruit of the tree in the centre, you shall not eat of it,
    you shall not touch it, lest you die.
But death has its beauty – an angel face – and death is
    fate. Man was never the immortal, never knew the god
as marble and pigment is known. The word of god,
    lest you die, may not be destiny. —Why do we pray?

169*

My world is the presence I find and make into figure and
    paint. This world is held in each eye of my twenty *ignudi*,
in their bodies and faces—bold, belonging, proud,
    truthful and strong; in men with passion for love and
    possession;
and in the knowledge that an ugly face does not diminish
    or denote. My Boaz, myself, my angelic boys' downright
    ugliness.
All born of earth bleed into decay, are bronzed, and cast
    as melody and song.

170

See my face. Do you love it? Not for its broken nose,
    thin lips, and chunky forehead
that frighten children before I speak. Judith took my head
    for her scowling, bearded grisly trophy
when I mistook myself as traitor, betrayer of God, failure
    of lovers, man of no consequence, merely potential.
My prophets and my Sibyls are built on rude creatures,
    repulsive, chubby thighed and podgy, *putti*

171

we love to lie about, to make believe are little angels:
    see their grimaces; selfish, seldom trusting yet
guardians of naming, and of the flow of knowledge from
    garden to the world.

Theirs are the transgressions of ugliness and death,
  the naive pretence, helplessness.
One or two stay the moment, apples on a tree before
  a storm.

172

What is this ugliness? Disturbing equanimity and serving
  notions where mirrors never quite satisfy?
My Boaz is ugly? Not to me. Here is a strong aged man
  whose long white beard and beak-like nose
call on you to watch, observe, to learn and love. Here
  within my reach is truth
and stern debate, in thought within my grasp, a me I can
  create in three dimensions to astound and magnify

173*

the cone, the staff, the knife, the hand that holds, the lime
  green cloth and pinkish hose
not snarling, just debating with myself: poor Bernard's
  bones are surely turning in his grave
that life should be so free, and smiles mistook for greed
  are no mere caricature.
So false the saintly odours we devise to smooth the way—
  it seems no truth exists without its painted halo.

174

Truth may seem simple line, harmonious curvature or
  stroke of delicate and feminine design;
it speaks too, indeed it shouts at times, from musculature
  and bone, from carved and polished stone, from
  roughened edge and ploughed field.
Close the distance to the eye, place the palm against the
  soil, toss and turn the chaff, for in the soundlessness
  between your strokes
and chisel taps there is another chrome, a node, a texture
  to the clay we are.

175

I find my truth in youthful conversation and autopsies,
    in flower and weed, in living bodies and decay of fruit.
Where do you find yours? In the heaven you pursue?
    In gold or land? In loving or in conquest and control?
All those silent sitting men and women, and my golden
    youth and manic warriors, and manikins
— my boys and girls in servitude to greater things I foist
    on this ceiling, the unblemished history of womb.

176*

But back to Boaz. Would you befriend this man and be his
    walking cane? Or pass him by
to worship at the door of fashion, high heels and silks that
    hide some bulging bountiful bewildered behemoth.
Give me St Anthony's grotesques, his monster scaly
    bodies, spikes and wings, horn and bat-like ears, long,
    suckered snouts.
There's beauty to be kissed and puckered, adorned with
    ram's horn and catapulted into bronzed battle spasm.

177

Holofernes, balls-naked on his bed, was most unfortunate
    that Judith took his eye, for she took his head too and
    trayed it to the people,
facing down Nebuchadnezzar with an artist's visage,
    arched at one corner of the universe, high and free.
On the other hand, David downs Goliath with a swift cast
    and then a slicing of his head. Empire is brought down
when the why is repossessed in a process of redemption.
    The eye of Zechariah reads the book.

178

My David awed the city and stands to me. He triumphs
    here with a gruesome stroke to sever heads
and prove the might of wisdom in the face of power
    corrupted and enlightened by the avarice of man.

But in the execution, David's posture is no more than that
    of everyman's possession of himself and for another.
Sacrifice is often not so generously answered by gods who
    relish in destruction, and let fate be.

179

Here is the risk for heroes and heroines, and spouse.
    To balance life with death and venture bravely to be
    beautiful;
to raise a brazen serpent that will heal the biting venom
    of snake and vermin; to cauterise and seal
night's uncertainty when light reveals its day decanted
    from some super centrifuge;
to be thirty days' in the coils and fangs of swarming
    question, rejection and submission; to survive.

180*

"O Florence, Florence, Florence. For your sins, for your
    brutality, your avarice, your lust, for your ambition
will fall on you many trials and tribulations." —
    Savonarola echoes in the labyrinthine ashes of the pit,
submits to his tradition, blooded in the scourge of Prato,
    of Cascina or the Centaurs, of the doomed in the flood:
all twisting bodies, foreshortened to extremity and truth,
    awash in oranges, greens and pinks;

181

things once beautiful, once bright and happy, watchful in
    the flow of light, now fearful of the consequences
for a world inhabited by wrinkled thought and crusted
    skin. Decaying in the absence of its love.
The thing abandoned hides in caves we never excavate,
    where mind and matter
blended to a soupy ether blindly wait the next creation.

Look at the skin

182

adam stirred
thought and said
look at the skin
touch the rising muscle
taste the fluid's wetnesses
rally the bone
hone your vision
tone your blood

183

be alone
in search of to belong
belong to be alone
enter the body

184

rest there
play there
love there
burn there

185

withdraw
to be again
without within
eyeball eyes
suck lips
tongue taste and tousle
palm your love
and tickle

in a muckle and a mickle
for nothing is fickle
nothing is fallow
nothing is everything
under the plough
bow in delight
bow in praise
bow to revisit
the sinbin
now

186

Four extremities that fight for life: the eye, the heart,
  the lung, the toe; and all desert my day. The dark is here.
Though I love night and seek to live there it becomes a
  where I cannot know. Deeply dark, so silent, heavy,
  densely ragged; a harsh and sullen blue.
I cannot hold or shape or colour change to flow the folds
  of errant cloak or comfort's blanket for the poorer eye.
Who goes there? I cry throughout its dull grasp. Who's
  there? I muddle in anger, lost and slowed by age-
  relentless bastard beau.

187

This young man brings great joy and all the pain we ask for.
  Urges body back to see inside the skin
its universal flush of birth, blossom, hand and breast.
  Energy finds days to remember for their truths.
Woman brings me through the body, conceives from every
  word I offer for possession of her presence,
intents I never phrased, and elegance of form. This mother—
  nurse-maid: Magdalene, Madonna, Eve, my owl
between night's thighs and silent eyes.

188

For she's with me, limbs still, languid; inviting darkness
    to embrace her and complete it.
I help her swollen breasts and abdomen to rise and fall,
    my testicles with Bacchus in his cups, swollen too,
    eyes glistening in the moon
that palms her stomach, firm and full with movements of
    the clay beneath; those slender rounded arms invite
    complicity
in what darkness might suggest or tolerate; night is where
    to bed the day, to wed the body, and to plant seed.

189

Adam stirred. His languid lonesome body withdrew his
    finger-reach to be with what he sensed about him.
He rose without disturbing air or god, and knew the onset
    of a spasm sparking from his fingertip that sped along
    his arm to belly, hip and spine;
one thigh stiffened down to calf, to toe and back again.
    Involuntarily. Muscles sudden in contraction and release
arrest shapes of earth beneath and sky above, and all things
    awaiting resurrection.

190

His flesh and sinew, hair and satin skin explode this waking
    seedburst. Mist washes underneath his blinking eyelids
and the world is made body. This is not what he has known
    before. There is enchantment at a palm pressing easily
    to his,
a mirror image not himself; some other. He stares at Eve
    whose now he knows as he is Adam, without need to
    wonder why.
He's not marooned. Bodies know; they tell their tale
    through form and touch, through colour and desire.
    What there is, is theirs.

191

Like powerful spotlights dancing on a distant hilltop or
    waving wall or cliffside over water, arms, palms and
    fingers
open breasts, chests and eyes, tilt chins, twitch thighs,
    then parting, come again to touch and dance
in a slow, deliberate encounter, teasing, testing, knowing
    their inevitable end.
Intensity warms the silken skin; hot muscle burns; in the
    groin a blushing brushing texture waits.

192

Bodies know. Their limbs entwine, taut as any ballet leap
    requires; their wholeness swells
to a rising sun, releases all the juices; in the taste of sweat
    and belly press, touch makes full
the petalled entrance to paradise untried; in trust each lilt
    of penis through vagina's open eye –
as one as one—again again – this long embrace voicing
    throats that do not need to learn. Language is no
    happenstance.

193

Here is invitation – Eve 'n Adam—penetration – vulva
    open to erection; risen nipples; hanging scrotum;
    nosing cheeks
all the open flesh and pleasured nerve-ends that had no
    need to speak, no need to draw on intellect
for sound enlightened throat, chest and ear – all
    mouthing understandings of intent.
Thrust on thrust, hip welding hip, skin seizing skin –
    the power is one.

194

Ejaculation and absorption of the seed is shared in this
    floating torso bonding; limbs,
abandoning fleshy gravity, turn in warm graceful arcs,
    and pulses of release, return again
creating for the universe an installation of intent:
    a sculptured motion, frescoed air, a poem of flesh,
without words to hinder the intensity or form its
    presence wills. Absence is no longer possible.

195

Now that bodies have discovered what they are, lovers of
    this universe in endless re-creation of itself,
all I believe seems lost as time abandons truth and death
    and revisits art in this making.
Beyond the so called honour and glory of God, what is
    there for me?
My great tomb for Julius lost, Moses triumphant, and my
    dying slaves and eerie crucifixions erect and offering
    the body of a Christ.

196

This open sesame, organic linear forever of the sculpted
    body in the firmament,
defining who we are and who we're not, the god we
    designate ourselves to be
so we can see, remote, powerful, close, dependent, and
    abstracted in the reality we wrap around the other.
Where do we find the self? In this mobile installation,
    unfixed and indeterminate, is species, is emotion in
    the making.

197

The body's fingerprint and all the pores unweave skin's
    linear reach into the far far away
where space is and place has no beginning. This silk
    unwoven body web lost its way

seeking synapse, a cleft, an excitation to recoil and curl
    and curdle it again to man and woman, muscle, bone
    and brain,
in silence. There is no one, no where, no other, no void;
    only the absence of existence we can recognise. —
    And me.

* * *

198

I awaken, shattering the emptiness, the flatness of the
    layered planes, angled, curved and jutting from the
    rock and clay I lie on.
My eyes fix distance, immobile, knowing. What happens
    then I cannot tell. Outside of my control
something from within urges upward from the belly to
    the chest and through a reflex swallow of the throat,
to swirl and boil in the cavity of mouth: this urge
    intensifies, waits until the head tilts high and lips
    rupture, wet and luscious, to release a solemn howl,
    a holiness ...

199

            —a clear and brilliant trumpet call,
            bel canto and *cadenza* to a sustained
                    high-pitched drone
                    echoing itself

200

                    And in that call
            — as liquids brew in blazing cauldrons,
                or seafoam, driven hard to shore
                    by wave and wind, scatters
            its throbbing clumps across a rocky outcrop —
                    some multiplicity of thought
                deep within the mound they lie on

vibrates to a maelstrom
round the copulating pair, birthing
herds of thrusting replicates that billow
in their myriads across the visible reach
of Eve-and-Adam's eye and mind.

201

En masse this wave's tumultuous flow
of ecstasy is pumped on to a climactic poise
and peak to then soften in a slow slow release
as bodies separate in satisfaction
and so, before a new awakening
all are ready now to sleep.

202

But as the universe insists
these myriads of man
become its messengers and elements
with immediate response to now—

203

Awake is how we live best.

204

I will return with things to tell
graffiti for a wall.
Farewell a while—Farewell.

205

For then they slept.

END OF BOOK 2

Book 3 — Standing On The Wall

(Verses 206-258)

MOVEMENT 24   *(Verses 206–211)*

Approach with confidence

206

Walls are best approached with confidence and readiness.
To puncture their illusionary power, the metaphysic.
Not on Berkeley's understanding alone;
    esse est percipi is fine and well until you try a header
    on stone.
In this wall of prophecy and presumption words are
    fixed. Flesh fouled and fallen, ribbed with indigestion,
    must redress itself with history's drumbeat
and the shape of words that make those things we think
    we know.

207

Naked we exit the mountain
    and naked we enter the valley.
    Must we return to the darkness?
Or search for the underground man
    drunken and dazzled by sunlight,
    who stumbles
and smashes his way

to the cliffs of thought
with a sense that somewhere within
are words that want to break free
from his vulvalus mouth.
I want to sing.
    I want to sing the body tune,
    the rhythms of blood,
    the living heart.

    208

I will begin up here, with the fall of darkness before sunrise,
    the heart of dawn pulsing night's embrace.
I want to sing. Here is a lung I can fill and file, leave a
    trace underneath folds of *cangiante*
and writhings of masks put on out of doors when we lurk
    behind vanity, snug in pretence.
Somewhere under the summer skin and the want of winter
    clothing is the whore sitting on seven mountains.

    209

                    The universe never lies?
                Is it what is, nothing else?
                    What we believe
                    —the sin of Eve,
                    the sun of Adam,
                    the christ crucified,
                the mother virgin young,
        the stones rolled back from gape of hell,
                a solemn bell clapping,
                    a song of songs,
                and walls—become
                notions of entitlement.
                    I prefer to work
                    then I dance
                    then I sing
        then I ride the road to Jericho and back
                    without a fall

210

or press on for Damascus. I hear the echoing rocks ask
    why—'Saul. Saul. Why persecutest thou me?'
Paint me in fresco with the fortitude of man, of the bodies we
    are. As stone from Pietrasanta and Carrara's bowels sing.
My fresco men will not fall from this wall like my great
    marble block fell from its mountain top
to shatter on the valley floor, bartering monumentalities
    that break backs, killing a man who sang.

211

Do I sit and ponder when walls need breaching or
    defence? Go, see what is and what can be; surrender
    only to your gut.
God fails to know the body we gave him to create.
    My body knows and knits its veins of fire with seams
    of liquid metal thread.
I would defend Florence. What is your defence? Hell has
    none; she is easily breached and quenched.
The wall is here, and not where your eyes and heart are
    but in a great spew of poisonous gullet, painted white
    to slay the landscape.

When is to be sufficient?

212

We have dreams to focus with, men and women to love,
  to hear, to write for and to paint.
When is to be sufficient? In the warmth of a child's smile
  or a welcoming wilderness for strangers?
Behind the generosity of our summer skins, and the
  warmth of winter clothing, there is always a route
to Prato, Gaza, Twin Towers — always a friend to stake and
  crush in the civilising of our insanity and need.

213

The mosquito drawing blood gets squashed and stains the
  finger tip with its life, a martyr to existence.
It already has offered new life to its host: death is not a
  requisite adventure. Who runs away may choose to
  fight again, or not.
The sword you pierce my baby with is of the finest steel,
  clean and sleekly loving in its kill. Is there a point to
  any death?
Paintbrush, trowel and chisel, quill, penis, parasol —
  all rise to herald yellow petals, red embrace.

214

Death seems neutral. A silent passage.
Whoever invented sin to measure life's worth and nudge
  us towards gated forests,
made calculations married to language we excrete for the
  burying of our dead. The god himself forgot and rested.
Adam had to eat the fig and find where he belonged — did
  he make music so that Eve might dance?

215

On this scaffolding my limbs risk notches that my boyhood
relished. Like my little chisels, I never hesitate to point
or turn.
The burning is not here. Nor is there a stool to squat upon
nearby. The wall that held the vault's west wing is gone.
All is open, rising careless of your needs.
Though I will fill your stories, chill your breath, steel
your spine, heat your bowels, fear will be out there.
What we do not want to know will tend towards debit,
diminish credit. You hanker for endorsement; will you
hunker to succeed?

216*

What is the point of death? Answer that, good suitor on
the cross. I see where it is, but why? To rut and then
to die?
'And will the flowers die?' a poet asks. There is purpose
and future in all we know, but not here. Disease has
logic, war has purpose, the cannibal nourishes ritual
and hunger.
Death is a zero point, nothingness. Unless, as pigments
infusing plaster, we are heterogeneous solutes in a
never saturated clay.
Entanglements of faith and reason dry like plaster, deny
ecstasy, leaving us to trawl skies for mackerel adrift
in foreign seas.

The wall is gone

217

The wall is gone—long stand the wall engendered,
    measured and triangulated in our dreams and wakings.
In its absence there is no anointed, nor any joy in
    resurrections, nor escape from fantasy.
In recovering dead flesh and long-forgotten bliss, in the
    unveiling of caves and penetration of darkness, sounds
    a bell.
Without the wall, the ecstatic of knowing will falter as
    absence becomes presence; and words cry out for
    metaphor.

218

From where else does Christ god come? his mother too
    and all his watching fathers? In the knowledge of the wall,
couched on wheels of pain, flayed skins, arrow heads, hell
    fire, breasts, snakes, Adam's finger, God's hand.
I am who am, where I am and why. This wall recognises me,
    lets me be its outside, its form and maker.
This condominium of personality is awaiting interchange,
    lurking by my ceiling, breaching boundaries of power,
    colour and relation.

* * *

219

When Jonah emerged from the belly to surface on wave and
    breathe freely of soft air and silence, he drank deeply
for beneath was time, above a skyway; nowhere could
    escape his eye.
He lay back to know it all, to tally what he was. No longer
    railing at what discomforted his honour,

he now owned fear and pain, knew openness, found voice
beyond the rhythms of the planet.

220

He was not crucified. If crucifixion so transforms as to
ennoble and endorse body and mind,
then, let me crucify myself to a worthy cross atop a
strident hill, and come, watch me from below.
For my mother is dead.
My father too.
I have offspring and siblings,
lovers and leavers of my own
to mourn and bury me in the tears that laughter might allow.

221

The dead are dead.
Though at times we will deny
corruption of the flesh, and our wishes' mirror neurons
may spill our stories across generations unborn. They
may as well be stillborn.
I lie here waiting the first nail, through my left palm.
The strike of iron crushing flesh and splintering bone
can be endured, the pain absorbed and known; but on the
second strike, this body will spasm and resist.

222

When all is done, feet bound, head pierced with darts of
thorn, side throbbing, leaking bloody flows
down this belly, matting pubic hair, as the light goes and
comes again and heartache weakly gathers,
there is this moment of relief, of ease, of thought,
of things seen, before death can dominate.
Might I too cry unbidden, rend the heaven's tapestry and
fill the sky with voice: My god, my god—
Eli, Eli lama sabachthani.

Fulfilling prophecy, revealing nothing

223

I will appoint counsel, listen to my body, answer questions:
    pain is knowledge; joy is understanding.
I see this body in twenty postures of power and loveliness,
    full of hope's energies. Full blooded,
magnificent aloft, and aware, each reveal is for a man who
    has come in glory with the morning sun
——my *ignudi*, angel Atlas full of grace and the soft delicacy
    of skin; flowing and still; their eyes waiting for coition's
bond do not weep for our slaughter.

224

    I cannot turn my eyes from hell's gate:
    but I can change my demons,
    tie them down, lock them in,
    and seeing instead the fires
    of intercourse in every flame, dive
    into its maw to course densing pools of passion.

225

    Mind absorbs the fear
    and lets the snake's open mouth behead
    where acorns bloom.
    Fragrance sculpts the pigment brush
    to shade thigh, brow or flowing hair or gown
    as ideas shaping words take form.

226

    Man will ride the body's flame,
    caress the mound,
    enter the cavern's watery ode and

clasp the rhythmic universal pulse.
Woman's open lips will purse to kiss
the welcome breath, knowing the season's
culture and her own strong spring.

227

Above the writhing pair, unseen but near the eye,
a detritus of soul and marrow overflows
like porridge oats infused with morning's milk,
ready to be savoured, salted and devoured.
But to what end?

228

A conundrum with or without the god which may or may
    not be the source we claim for evil,
our universe morphs into shadow lounges of bustle,
    colourful, noisy, and riven by clocks
for arrivals, departures, delays and cancellations and ever
    refreshening schedules of judgement.
We draft, draw, drive or drag ourselves onto a mesh of
    gateways; skyward for completion, satisfaction—
    deification.

229

If there is no future and only a shady past, all already is.
    This expanding present is merely generational—
    fulfilling prophecy, revealing nothing.
In perfume's golden bowl with blood smell in our wake
    we swim or float, easy in the soupy oil,
eager to array motives with indulgence untouched by pole
    or spin. Where we massage our bodies
to absorb the soporific, we taste aromas to endure, close
    our eyes to see what is hidden in stone we cannot cut.

230

What do we see? Dignity dissolved, abnegation, relation,
   the lack of bile, a new son?
In Charon's skiff, we watch that goat-like face, the burning
   eyes, but sit quietly by gunwales waiting
to be deep-freezed in the gut of ambiguity. Though like a
   seagull rising from a rocky foreshore, our fear of silence
wings seaward with a willingness to let go—confronting
   darkness, storm or hungry whales, our instinct is infinity.

231

If all we want is half a loaf, a palace seems inappropriate.
   Less promise, and simpler direction may navigate routes
to absence we can cope with and accept without fable.
   My fist clutching for release may be just that, or not.
The ground you plant me in, the drill you harrow clean,
   the ashes that you rake and package for a mantlepiece
   or attic, these
bring confirmation of sentiment, not of understanding.
   One story ends and other tales wag.

232

If we give to friend or stranger and we trust the 'goad of
   flesh', arrows for the mind,
perhaps heaven is adoration of knowledge, and god is
   who we know ourselves to be.
The face behind the stone that slants atop this ridge,
         doesn't know my shadow imprint
           on its knarled exterior,
              mapped and coloured
                by its lichens.
I grow here, embossed and calcified by time and absence.
   It is how, why and where I will remember.

Where presence infinitely sits

233

Time is a growing past: there is no now. Beauty is resolved
and we verify our attachment to the clay time made,
the clay man kneaded, coloured, picked and pointed,
brushed and scuffed across this monument to fable,
rebinding dialogues and grammars in our own skins,
re-telling, for centuries of stray watchers, disciplinarians
and popinjays,
the truths reached and sliced open clean as a breakfast
apple, unafraid to see the core, the marinade.

234

Strip away your name.
Strip away your face.
Strip away your voice,
each piece of clothing,
those elegant shoes.
Strip every detail from your skin,
strip back
each muscle to the bone,
each bone to marrow.
What then?
Nothing left to quantify.
Are you, too, absent, or is absence
where your presence infinitely sits
in contemplation?
Only the remnants of crucifix—trunk, crossbar, nails and
twisted thorn-branch in the distance.
Embodied on high where the eye sites it – worshipful and
beautiful – the fulcrum, the measure, the point – the
who-is-not who is. —Swear.

235

As he leaned his body back — so near to the void beneath
  his scaffolding,
the figure he was painting stirred before him. The porcelain
delicacy of skin, the intense ochre lurking underneath
  blue eyes,
her bare waist and naked loins, mirroring his lustre of
reflection.

236

He knew the richness, knew the risk, the courage and the
  pain — but lifted the flatness
from each pigment with his brushes. She was nobility,
  she was charm, strength,
and meditation. As he acted to his thought, she birthed
  for her maker.
Inevitable entanglements of her belief and his gave art
  and reason much to do.

237

His brushes spread the iridescent flesh; and its absorption
  warmed her blood
and freshened up the morning. The whites that overlay
  her arms and thighs, burnished skin
as on polished marbled virgins, and filled the open sky
  of lapis lazuli
with the wonder of humanity, and with jealousy and fear.

238

  Below the gaping mouths of hell are new
    caves to wander in
    the night, awaiting
    shipments of pigmented souls
  embodied in
    the ghastly smiles of Charon's phantom
    men, rejects of holiness, purchased

at markets in Sodom or Gomorrah;
—our visions do not hesitate to spin
the wheels of luck and walk away.
We are alone and all our smiles will not
undo the shackle we so readily pass on;
—our sanctity is rich in poisoned pollinates
and cross-legged stools; one riddle
answers all but leaves
the blind dancing on scaffolds.

Dance we will

239

Already in the path of transition, word is made flesh
　　underneath the plaster, intonaco and layers of brick.
I trust myself and polish until the world softens to a
　　youthful effervescence.
So, dance we will, sculpting sensuous shifts of form and
　　mass as higher on this wall myriads are climbing,
　　limned in bright amazement at the day that's come,
confident in scaffold, wall, pigment and brush; all pounced,
　　incised and ready for coition to attach fertility to our
　　invasion of eternity.

240

—See. Here he comes rising as if borne on air, arms raised,
　　stepping up; aglow, unveiling darkness.
This bright man and his pliant mother acolyte embrace
　　the spellbound horde which has its eye fixed
on far horizons. But drawn inexorably in anticlockwise
　　buoyancy, and filled with the pulse of promise
in this swirling cascade, each stills their moment as the
　　where they know as wall dissolves.

I think of Michelangelo

241*

A mind aroused by great excitement speaks itself: '*Behold,
I am the handmaid of the Lord. Be it done to me
according to your word...*'
Then, silence, streaming through, eases the roughness and
ungainly stagger of his thighs and shoulders, softening
his body.
His shagginess still breathes authority and strength,
his stillness, elegance and inclination.
With the power and tension of a Parthenon unsprung,
released into its sky, momentum opens hidden springs
of light and dark.

242

I see it too – my hand and brush seem deep inside the
surface of the wall. I lean into the future I create
without a sound,
scaffolding that held me crumples underneath and
disappears, and I am left to fall forward, inward
as if gravity itself re-bore its gut to let me float in space,
move into the blues and whites of sky,
and all around me gusting shoals of life entangle limb and
belly, trunk and flowing hair.

243

Movement is what there is, calving each momentum's
endless turning,
a slow relentlessness of coiled confident excitement
humming its mighty power, its own expansive curving
song. This is the body that it knows.
Strange figures in a multitude of poses animate as far in
each direction as the eye may see.

244

We are in it too; laughing, loving, sexing, knowing and
    abandoning. As if there is no more but this.
I think of Michelangelo. And see the scaffold fall, the wall
    dissolve in me and disappear as he floats wild
with flailing arms and legs dancing a fresco in the sky he
    made for me. I follow.
There is nowhere else to go. Nothing else to be. No one
    else to love. Just me. And what I think I see.

245

That world I think I see fills and draws the soft wells of
    wall, absorbs the body's flesh and blood;
bones no longer needed to sustain muscle and mind
    dissolve to fluid's integrity and mass.
Flesh and bone have no need of speech; fingers that once
    caressed lips of love are now the love of lips
so far beyond their comprehension, that thought,
    no longer necessary to know, becomes a mucus and
    sweetness of the well.

246

The well too frames the darkened deep, the flooding mist,
    binding and bounding every thing there is,
chair, man, woman; laptop or confession box; cowls, skills,
    images of art; mathematics; games that children play.
Here is new, strange, colourful and white, soundless yet
    abuzz to the beat of bass drum heaves and tinkling
    cymbal wheels;
here is an opening, yawning, yawing, loaming, gleaming,
    formless and unfathomable idea—a word without the
    flesh to speak it.

247

The threshold we cross is adamant, *lignum vitae* coated
    in oils and creams to melt the toughness of the flesh
    we are
and sleep us through its border wavelengths where
    consciousness and nothingness coalesce in perpetual
    hovering
where sound hums its rush of knowledge to coil and recoil
    like octopuses washed by invisible tow of wavetide
across the floor of oceans. Lungs brace to the visionary
    breathing of a drowning soul.

248

Soul. That word. It frightens children—and old painter
    sculptors weakened by the weight of brush or mallet. Soul.
Nothing knows its place. The heart, breast, brain. The inner
    eye. The breath we expire at death out of one mould
    into some other place.
What vital breath this is, the last, expended for
    measurement, for chemical analysis of its constituent
    malodours, for final judgement and re-placement
in alcoves hid in paradise or hell, purgatory or limbo.
    —Or, this finality, expired into a nothingness we each
    possess. Dead is dead.

When sound converts to silence

249

And then, silence? Silence so full and rounded, utterly
  immobile, the emptiness of voided space
as during a play of dazzling skill, when momentarily a
  stadium roar is quenched;
and a strike swings every eye to the rising ball high into
  the firmament —
each throat closed, every foot still, no breeze blows,
  no bird sings. Nothingness has rooted deep, seductive
  and motionless.

250

Fathoms inside the skull, presence prevails: visceral and
  salutary, tickling
exhaustion, exhilaration, expectation; possessive,
  seasoned by a soupcon of there-ness.
The images that fill the vault and wall, and reach past the
  architecture of sky and sea, embrace perception far
  beyond our sun, moon and planets.
The earth's crust holds to our feet as if marking its
  presence to this moment of transition when sound
  converts to silence.

251

  I was deep inside, clenched, clamped, covering and
    covered,
      the embodiment of resurrection, of word made flesh,
      of song singing its climax
      of creation, and of flood.
    Into your body I place mine   into my body I bring
      yours

two as one is one;
our sum remains   a zero of thought that is not.
When, where our flesh peaks and surrenders   to
     release,
     we can forget ourselves;
there is an undressed formless absence.

252

Is this the aureole of Nyx, night of origins, daughter of
     chaos, birthing sleep and death in veiled cold arms,
sucking, suckling and indulging, willing to await
     manhood's return to penetrate
where destiny's open maw entertains no exception.
The mind acknowledges the dense mass
of slow carved *contrapposto*, the textured streaks,
     as yellow-red devour the azure, and sky disappears.

253

               Somewhere somewhy somehow
          behind the vaulting mass of a distant now
               other stuff is happening
atoms tuning, charges building, blocks of space renewing
     in a quantum bowl of particle and force, stirring
     fusion, churning in some mindspelling stirabout

254

          guarantors perhaps of passing thought
               and sculptor's chisel
          of painter's brush and poet's word

255

               ... and—Michelangelo?
     absorbed in the great womb of chaos he created
          leaving us to falter, wonder, and pass on
               for we know   nothing

256

—a sigh, in slow
perturbance
dehiscence

257

another dance is coming,
no slouching beast
or new vault to follow
the wall's collapse, its dissolution

258

our end is an endless in-breath
to fill — to vitalise
and imperceptibly
to let go—
never to know

THE END

Notes to the Poem Text

(Indicated in text by asterisk on relevant movement or verse number)

Prologue

MOVEMENT 1*: *The Gaze* (verses 1-5)

Based on a ceiling image which I labelled for myself 'The Gaze'. This seated female figure is in a spandrel above the 'Jesse-David-Salomon' lunette. One of the series depicting the forty generations of the ancestors of Christ.

Verse 3: The 'young man' is one of Michelangelo's *Ignudi*, (a word he coined from nudo / naked) twenty male nude youths seated in counterpoint pairs on plinths surrounding the ceiling panels.

The Libyan Sibyl, one of Michelangelo's most beautifully expressive and dynamic images, is nearby. The five Sibyls and seven Prophets are all painted larger than life size in frames of 390 cm × 380 cm (c. twelve and a half feet square)

Book 1 Creation Part I: Creation's hold
(verses 6-64)

MOVEMENT 2: *The force that floats through me* (verses 6-12)

Verse 6: Michelangelo depicts the creator's buttocks and the soles of his feet as God speeds through the firmament creating the sun, moon and plants. The artist wrote of his cramped conditions on the high platform, but he did not have to lie on his back to fresco the ceiling!

MOVEMENT 4: *As dark and light disperse* (verses 24-34)

Verse 29: '.. virginal blue, pinpricked with silver's gold': The ceiling had been painted simply as a blue sky with gold stars prior to Michelangelo's work.

Verse 30: The prophet Jonah is a dominant figure on the ceiling, seated high over the altar, observing creation.

MOVEMENT 5: *I too begin with scaffolding* (verses 35-41)

Verse 35: Michelangelo's first demand on arrival in the chapel was for the removal of a scaffolding and platform built for him by the Vatican architect, Bramante. That it hung from the ceiling he was about to fresco angered the painter who then engineered his own platform, astounding all with his original design which left the ceiling surface free of impediment.

MOVEMENT 6: *The flowing moon* (verses 42-48)

Verse 47: The 'Blasket island bull': a reference to an Irish tale that the islanders ferried the island bull to a nearby small uninhabited island to isolate him from their cows; but the intervening sea didn't prevent him from swimming back.

MOVEMENT 7*: *In the grip of the uncanny* (verses 49-59)

Also references Michelangelo's 'The Rape of Ganymede' drawn later (in the 1530s) for his beloved young nobleman, Cavalieri.

Book 1 Creation Part II:
In the mirror of creation's dust
(verses 65-116)

MOVEMENT 10: *The cartoon will draw itself* (verses 68-82)

Verse 70: 'I need men to do my bidding' – Michelangelo, who saw himself as a sculptor, not a painter, took the Sistine Ceiling job reluctantly under Papal pressure. He had not done fresco work since leaving the Lorenzo de' Medici sculpture garden training 'school' so he needed to re-learn the skills. He employed assistants from Florence, is home city. They were well known to him from his youth, some were later work colleagues, some friends: all experts whose work he admired and trusted.

Verse 73: 'I need a certain amount of pretty blues...' is a phrase from a letter by Michelangelo to Fra Jacopi di Francisci in May 1508, Barocchi and Ristori, *Il carteggio di Michelangelo* (Florence, 1965) Vol 1, p. 74, quoted in *The Sistine Chapel: A Glorious Restoration*, Ed. P de Vecchi, page 49.

Verse 75: '... who now will rescue Mordecai?/ Who will be his Haman, crucified, not hanged?' – Haman is shown crucified, punishment for his betrayal. Haman is chief minister to Xerxes, King of Persia whose Jewish wife is Esther. She reveals that Haman plans to eradicate the Jews and hang her uncle, Mordecai. Instead, the king hangs Haman. Michelangelo decides to portray him as crucified (Zöllner, p.192). It brought to my mind another Mordecai, (Mordecai Vanunu, an Amnesty International prisoner of conscience), born an Israeli Jew, kidnapped in Rome, tried and imprisoned in 1986 by Israel, who is today (although having completed his eighteen year prison sentence) still denied his freedom for revealing the truth about the secret military nuclear programme which Israel had lied about for decades.

Verse 82: 'This fresco lark/ is not an art/ for an old man's bone' echoes Michelangelo's own thoughts as expressed in several of his some extant 300 sonnets and madrigals, many of significant quality and highly regarded by his peers and contemporaries.

MOVEMENT 11: *Beneath the hard breath of a curious god*
(verses 83-88)

Verse 84: 'forty marble notions' – Michelangelo had spend eight months selecting and supervising and cutting marble blocks at the Carrara marble quarries for shipping to Rome to be used in making the forty figures for the commissioned tomb of Julius II, the pope who commissioned the ceiling fresco. This tomb and the contract for producing it became major and unhappy issues throughout the artist's life. Only a very much reduced and simpler tomb was ultimately created, but which included his great 'Moses' sculpture (see below, Movement 20 notes)

MOVEMENT 12: *Such beauty and its solitude are radical*
(verses 89-100)

Verse 90: Michelangelo wrote a sonnet, dedicated to a Giovanni da Pistoia (as yet unidentified) which is echoed here. He also sketched a cartoon, preserved in Florence, of himself at work

on the ceiling. He writes, 'I've got myself a goitre from this strain' and 'My belly's pushed by force beneath my chin. / My beard toward Heaven, I feel the back of my brain / Upon my neck, I grow the breast of a Harpy; / My brush, above my face continually, / Makes it a splendid floor by dripping down. / ...
... ... And I am bending like a Syrian bow.' (quoted and illustrated by Zöllner, pp 76-77)

MOVEMENT 13: *Why I find it in my mind to paint* (verses 101-112)

Verse 101: On the ceiling panel, Adam and Eve leave Eden at the point of an angel's sword, bowed and haggard, suddenly aged, no longer the youthful vigorous and beautiful couple who sported beneath the tree. The image is structured as a double arch: its centre pillar, the tree, is entwined by the serpent who reaches forbidden fruit to Eve. She's to the left with Adam standing and forming the left pillar of the archway; her sensuous lips turned now towards the serpent are aligned to Adam's penis. On the right hand side of this panel then, the departing now aged couple mirror this, arched by the angel who reaches or points over them with his menacing sword.

Verse 105: Noah appears on three panels of the nine on the ceiling, the first to be painted, the last in the chronology of creation. Firstly, Noah's sacrifice of sheep, oxen and other creatures, a celebratory ritualistic image of submission, and acknowledgment. Then, the flood and the ark. And finally, the drunken naked Noah and his three naked sons standing over him: mankind's new state perhaps, which also includes a man, Noah presumably again, at work digging the soil in the garden outside with a spade.

MOVEMENT 14: *The centrifuge — forms I can release*
(verses 113-116)

Verse 116: See Michelangelo's phrase 'my lame gait' in a poem on page 148 in *Michelangelo: Life, Letters, and Poetry*, Trans. George Bull & Peter Porter (OUP, 2008 edition). 'Hence love walks with a limp,' he writes in another poem, No. 30 p 108, in *The Poetry of Michelangelo: an annotated translation*, James M. Saslow (Yale UP 1991).

Book 2 Eternal Day —The Work

(verses 117-205)

MOVEMENT 18: *Excitements of transience* (verses 135-142)

Verse 135: Michelangelo's own images for his condition on the scaffold, from his poem — see above note in Movement 12, verse 90.

Verse 140: *Terribilità* – a wonderful word – was a quality attributed to Michelangelo by his contemporaries. It refers to the 'awesomeness or emotional intensity of conception and execution in an artist or work of art' (*Shorter Oxford English Dictionary*).

MOVEMENT 19*: *I have my own work to do* (verses 143-149)

References to ceiling images here include: Zechariah, the first great figure of a prophet, over the entrance door; to right and left, scenes include Goliath, and Judith with the head of Holofernes; the first great ceiling panel, the Drunkenness of Noah; the sibyl Delphica and prophet Joel flank that panel.

Verse 148: Michelangelo was indeed at times a bridge builder and creator of effective military installations for the defence of Florence.

Verse 149: The cold winter wind – the *tramontana* from the Alps – could make the *intonaco* too cold for painting, or if it froze, the colours would not absorb properly and flaked. This, and a mildew fungus, caused Michelangelo great frustration in the initial months of work when whole sections of painted fresco were affected. Sangallo, an experienced frescoist who was the Pope's architect and Pope Julius insisted he carry on however.

MOVEMENT 20: *I had this dream* (verses 150-161)

Verse 150: Carrara (and Pietrasanta) quarries provided the marble for most of Michelangelo's sculptures. He worked there as early as 1498 (aged 23) quarrying marble for his most famous Pieta, this at the time that Savonarola (see note to verse 180), the fire-and-brimstone preaching friar, was hanged in Florence's *Piazza della Signoria*, and his corpse burned in a bonfire, his ashes thrown into the Arno river.

Moses, one of his greatest sculptures, was carved for the never fully realised tomb of Julius. Twenty five years later, in 1542, Michelangelo changed his mind about the angle of the figure's head and re-carved it, and the figure's legs, in situ, a remarkable feat of craftsmanship. 'The motives were certainly of an artistic nature, but the presence of the Altar of Chains on the opposite side of the transcept from *Moses* may have influenced the decision to turn the prophet's head. The altar was the very symbol of Catholic superstition and the foundation of that temporal power that continues to uphold a Church in which Micehelangelo no longer believed.' See Forcellino, *Michelangelo: A Tormented Life*, page 219-220 (Polity Press, 2009).

MOVEMENT 21: *Until we discover the next word*   (verses 162-164)

Verse 162: Bacchus: sculpted by Michelangelo in 1496-97; this classical figure is controversial for its depiction of an inebriated, almost staggering figure, with a rounded feminine body rather than a classically proportioned male 'god'. '... an expression of dissoluteness the most revolting' wrote Shelly in 1820, echoing many contemporaries of the sculptor. Self-indulgent and anti-classical in mood perhaps but most venturesome – carved just one year before Michelangelo created his most famous *Pieta*.

Verse 163: Laocoön: legendary masterpiece of Greek classical sculpture, re-discovered in 1506 underground in a Roman vineyard. Michelangelo was one of the first informed and invited to inspect it. Laocoön, a Trojan priest in the temple of Posidon, warned Troy against the wooden horse: '*Timeo Danaos et dona ferentes*' (Beware of Greeks bearing gifts), in Virgil's *Aeneid*. The sculpture portrays the priest and his two sons being strangled to death by two serpents as a punishment by the gods. Michelangelo echoed its postures in some of his *ignudi* on the ceiling.

MOVEMENT 22: *The matter is temptation*   (verses 165-181)

Verse 169: Boaz: spelled as Booz on the ceiling fresco label, Boaz is among the ancestors of Christ, and is described as 'ugly' and 'quarrelsome' by most commentators. In the Talmud and Midrash, Boaz was a rich landowner, a judge, a prince of the people, pious, learned and just. Legend has it he lost all his sixty children in his lifetime. At eighty, he got married (to Ruth who conceived his child) and died the day after the wedding. Michelangelo's interest in 'ugliness' may well stem from his own stated lack of physical beauty...'I see myself so ugly,' he says in one poem, and compares himself to a scarescrow in another, mentioning also that he spits, snores, farts and loses teeth! Condivi writes of his flattened nose, square forehead, thin lips and scanty eyebrows! For more, see pages 249-250, Ross King, *Michelangelo and the Pope's Ceiling* (Chatto & Windus, London, 2002)

Verse 173: 'Poor Bernard's bones': St Bernard of Clairvaux (1090-1153) preached (recruited) energetically — 'Cursed be he who does not stain his sword with blood — and with great success for the Second Crusade but thus bore responsibility for its failure.' He denounced Peter Abelard, and was a combater of heresy. Dante Alighieri's *Divine Comedy* includes him in the final book (*Paradiso*, cantos XXXI–XXXIII), a poem Michelangelo knew intimately.

Verse 176: 'St Anthony's Grotesques': refers to the engraving, 'The Temptation of St Anthony' by Martin Schongauer (c. 1470), a powerful work of fantasy in the then new medium of etching. It portrayed a demonic assault on the holy saint in a phantasmagoria of bazaar, exciting imagery. When about 13 or 14 years old, Michelangelo drew a 'perfect pen-and-ink copy' of this, and also translated the engraving into a colourful painting that 'crackles with visual imagery' (the surviving 1487/1488 work is attributed to Michelangelo by some, denied by others).

Verse 180: Girolamo Savonarola (1452-1498), best known for instigating the 'bonfire of the vanities' in Florence, was the renown fire-and-brimstone Dominican preacher of his time. He ran foul of the authorities eventually, was arrested, tortured, hanged and his body was burned in public in Florence. Michelangelo retained all his life a childhood echo of Savonarola's 'living voice', on matters of theological and philosophical debate on the nature of human life, on man's relation to God, on sin, especially the sin of sodomy, and on salvation of the soul. The quotation, 'O Florence, Florence ... ... tribulations' is quoted in Ross King, *Michelangelo and the Pope's Ceiling*, p. 86 (source: R Redolfi, *Life &Time of Girolamo Savonarola*, trans. G Greyson (Routledge, 1959).

Prato: in 1512 there was a slaughter of several thousand of its citizens by the army of Pope Julius II in his expansion of the Papal States. The Battle of Cascina in 1364 between the troops of Florence and Pisa, resulted in victory for Florence and the death of a thousand Pisans, with two thousand more captured. Michelangelo did preparatory drawings of the subject which survive, and a complete cartoon of the composition, but the painting was never completed.

Book 3 Standing on the Wall
(verses 206-258)

MOVEMENT 25: *When is to be sufficient?*   (verses 212-216)

Verse 216: 'And will the flowers die?' From 'Poem from a three-year old' by Brendan Kennelly (in *Irish Poems for Young People*, Cashman & Quinn ed. Wolfhound Press 1974, et seq.)

MOVEMENT 30: *I think of Michelangelo*   (verses 241-248)

Verse 241: 'Parthenon unsprung': The notion of a Parthenon 'unsprung' derives from this paragraph by John W. Dixon Jr (in his essay entitled 'Theology and Form: Reflections in the Spaces of the Imagination', *JAAR, xlv 2 Supplement*, June 1997). It follows his statement that the Parthenon is a 'dangerous' building, and proceeds to explain:

'The Parthenon has been tamed and rationalized into an image of Greek sobriety and balance and harmony, a cold image from 18th century neo-classicism. But the Parthenon is more, and more terrible. It is the center, the link between earth and sky, the mountain and the sea. It is lifted up in masculine authority but below in the flank of the hill is the female cave of the fates. It is the cool harmony and balance of geometric order. But every line is slightly curved, stretching slightly with the energy of life within. Tremendous power is gathered just under control. It is the power of Achilles or Alcibiades, the awesome power of animal strength combined with human intelligence and no moral control. It is the power and energy that made the history of Greece, the grim, prideful, terrible history of Greece. But once, in the actuality of this image, Greeks achieved control of power. The awesome intelligence of Athena, the mother-ruler who brought forth the olive by the shore of the sea, the power of the woman born of man and not of the soft and drifting foam of the sea, that singular intellectual power brought the terrible energy under control. And there it rests, on the hill in sight of the sea. Those who truly look at it are, for a time, in the presence of the gods.'

Glossary of Terms

Cangianti

Translates as 'colour change'; the use of colour variation to create form (such as folds, drapings, etc) and texture in for instance a garment.

Cartoon

An initial full sized drawing on heavy paper, often quite large sheets, which is then placed on the freshly plastered area to be frescoed; the outlines of figures, etc are transferred to the plaster by means of incision (knife stab through to the plaster), or 'pounced' – dabbed along the outlines which have been pierced with pin holes. A small muslin or similar cloth bag of charcoal creates an outline of black dots on the plaster. No cartoons for the ceiling still exist among the over 500 surviving drawings and sketches by Michelangelo (who had a pile of '*chartoni*' from his Rome studio burned by an assistant – a loss of 'what must have been among the most wonderful drawings ever made' (Martin Gayford, *Michelangelo: His Epic Life*, (Penguin/Figtree 2013).

Contraposto

In the visual arts, a sculptural scheme, used by the ancient Greeks, in which the standing human figure is poised with the weight on one leg, freeing the other which is bent at the knee. With the weight shift, the hips, shoulders, and head tilt, suggesting relaxation as well as movement that denotes life. Used for draped as well as nude figures, fluidity and ease of the *contrapposto* pose enlarged the expressive possibilities of figure sculpture. Michelangelo introduced tension by pushing one limb forward and another back—thrusting an arm forward over a receding leg, for instance. His 'David' deeply influenced later sculptors. He used *contrapposto* with great effect in his ceiling paintings, particularly in the *ignudi* paired figures.

Giornata

What can be plastered and painted in one day (plural: *giornate*). The wet plaster dries through the day so time is a major controlling factor. *Buon* Fresco is painting on wet plaster. Fresco can also be done '*a secco*' (when the plaster is dry). Michelangelo favoured the former as the true fresco.

Ignudi

The 'twenty naked youths' on the ceiling panels which Michelangelo called '*Ignudi*' are masterful portrayals of the human body in a variety of complex poses, beautiful, sensual, and without flaw. their nakedness establishes the significance of the body in itself and in its role on the ceiling where man has been created naked, beautiful and whole, without need of covering, self-contained and complete. Art historians Gabriele Bartz and Eberhard König have said of the *Ignudi*: 'There is no image that has had a more lasting effect on following generations than this.'

Intonaco

The top layer of plaster essential to fresco (fresh) painting. The *intonaco* (calcium hydroxide) was a layer of fresh (wet) plaster laid on an underlay of dry plaster (called *arriccio*). Made from sand and heated limestone or marble, the *intonaco* was mixed to a smooth paste and needed skilled masons to lay and trowel to a thickness of a half-inch. It provided the permeability to absorb pigments and seal them into the masonry as it dried. One day's work — a *giornata* — was determined by this drying process as painting had to be completed before the plaster got too dry. Cartoons were fixed to the wet plaster to outline the drawings by pouncing or making incisions through the paper.

Pentimenti

The elements of correction or re-touching the artist decides on after the fresco is essentially completed; perhaps additional detailing of highlights and shadows, and other fine-tuning for instance of eyes and eyelashes, etc.

Pozzolana

The local materials used in Rome for the *intonaco* plaster or mortar fresco layer were crushed and powdered limestone, tufa, a soft stone, and pozzolana, a volcanic rock. Pozzolana was ideal material as it fixed the colour pigments deep into the wet plaster.

Bibliography: a short listing

This is a list of some works which proved of particular interest during my research and background reading. There were in addition numerous general works and scholarly articles on various online sites, wide ranging in theme, some of which are mentioned in the Notes. In particular, the excellent philosophical and critical writings on art, religion, spirituality in the works of Michelangelo's Sistine Ceiling and Last Judgment Wall by the late Professor John F Dixon (whose *The Christ of Michelangelo* was published by the University Press of America, 1994).

Illustrated

Zöllner, Frank, Christopher Thoenes, Thomas Popper. *Michelangelo 1475 – 1564: Complete Works*. Directed and produced by Benedickt Taschen. Taschen GmbH, Koln, 2007. Illustrated. Scholarly texts, detailed extensive notes and superb image reproductions.

De Vecci, Piereluigi, General Editor. Diana Murphy, English-language Edition Editor. *The Sistine Chapel: A Glorious Restoration*. Essays presented at a conference at the Vatican 31 March 1990. Abradale Press, Harry N. Abrams, Inc., New York 1994. A co-production with NTY Nippon TV Network Corp., Tokyo. Illustrated.

Partridge, Lauren W. with texts by Gianluigi Colalucci and Fabrizio Manchinelli, trans by Lawrence Jenkins. Foreword by Dr. Francesco Buranelli. Michelangelo: *The Last Judgment, A Glorious Restoration*. Photographs by Takashi Okamura. Abradale Press, Harry N. Abrams, Inc. Publishers, New York 1997. Illustrated.

Néret, Giles. *Michelangelo, 1475–1564: Universal Genius of the Renaissance*. Taschen GmbH, Koln, 2010. Illustrated.

Biography

Condivi, Ascanio. *Life of Michelangelo Buonarroti* (1553). Translated by Charles Holyroyd, 1911. See also under 'Poetry' below, George Bull, editor.

Forcellino, Antonio. *Michelangelo: a Tormented Life*. Translated by Allan Cameron. Polity Press, Cambridge, 2009/2010. (First Italian edition, 2005)

Gayford, Martin. *Michelangelo: His Epic Life*. Fig Tree Penguin Books, London 2013.

Vasari, Giorgio. *Lives of the Artists: The Life of Michelangelo* (1550 & 1568). Various translations available.

Poetry

Bull, George, Editor, translations by George Bull & Peter Porter. *Michelangelo: Life, Letters, and Poetry*. With Introduction and Notes by George Bull. Oxford University Press, 1987.

Nims, John Frederick, Translator. *The Complete Poems of Michelangelo*. University of Chicago Press, 1998, 2000.

Saslow, James M. *The Poetry of Michelangelo: An Annotated Translation*. Yale University Press, 1991.

Miscellaneous

Blech, Benjamin & Roy Doliner. *The Sistine Secrets: Unlocking the Codes on Michelangelo's Defiant Masterpiece*. JR Books, London, 2008.

Graham-Dixon, Andrew. *Michelangelo and the Sistine Ceiling*. Weidenfelt & Nicolson, London 2008.

Hall, James. *Michelangelo and the Reinvention of the Human Body*. Chatto & windus, London, 2005.

King, Ross. *Michelangelo and The Pope's Ceiling*. Chatto & Windus, London, 2002.

Acknowledgments

My thanks to the many people who provided support in various ways during the time I spent working on this poem: my family of course, and especially my daughter Soracha whose penchant for wild thought and enthusiastic discussion and innovation was wonderfully generative, and my brother Michael (Fr. Mike); colleagues and friends who gave generous time to reading and discussion of the work at various stages and drafts, early or late. Among these are Siobhan Campbell, Tom Conaty, Angeline Hampton (A. A. Kelly), Maurice Harmon, Maighread Medbh, Andrew Phillips (formerly of The British Library), Mary Swander Poet Laureate of Iowa, U.S.A.).

Kalichi Donohue for his coaching mentorship and preparatory work for the audio recording of the poem, for his audio editing and embellishments and to Jason Varley, sound engineer and to the Soundwave Studio, Blackrock Co Louth.

The filmmaker Peter Salisbury of FOTOEIRE who ventured on an innovative poetry film, *Poetry from the Wall* based on *The Sistine Gaze*, and to poets Tom Conaty, Daragh Bradish, Paul Bragazzi, and Nessa O'Mahony for their participation.

Ray Lynn for coordinating production of a limited illustrated hand-bound edition and Susan Waine for design and layout (for The OtherWorld Press: ISBN 978-0-9576854-5-1: info@otherworld.ie) and the artist Mary T. Kearns whose 21 images include a cover image painted in *buon* fresco.

The editors of these journals in which extracts from the poem have appeared: *Axon: Creative Explorations* (online journal, http://www.axonjournal.com.au) University of Canberra, Australia, edited by Paul Hetherington; *About Place Journal: a literary online journal* Vol II, Issue II (http://aboutplacejournal.org), edited by Michael McDermot, at the Black Earth Institute, Wisconsin, U.S.A. *Census: Seven Towers Anthology* 2013; The Blue Max Review, Rebel Poetry, Cork (2013); Gene Barry's Blackwater Poetry online, 2014.

Finally, special thanks to my publisher, Jessie Lendennie, founder of Salmon Poetry, and her team, especially Siobhán Hutson for her professionalism, artistry and production expertise.

Poet and publisher SEAMUS CASHMAN founded the Irish literary publishing house Wolfhound Press in 1974 where he remained publisher until 2001. He has three published poetry collections: *Carnival* (Monarchline 1988), *Clowns & Acrobats* (Wolfhound Press, 2000), and *That morning will come: new and selected poems* (SalmonPoetry, 2007). He co-edited the now classic anthology, *Irish Poems for Young People* (1975, 2000); and in 2004 compiled the award-winning *Something Beginning with P: new poems from Irish poets* (The O'Brien Press). He was one of three English language judges (with Yusef Komunyakaa and Debjani Chatterjee) for the first International Mamilla Poetry Festival in Ramallah, Palestine in 2013, and edited its English language anthology. A poetry workshop facilitator, he has given poetry readings in Ireland, England, Wales, the UK, Belgium, Saudi Arabia and in Iowa and Wisconsin, USA. He is an emeritus International Fellow at the Black Earth Institute (USA), where he edited the 'Peaks & Valleys' issue of their *About Place* online arts journal. He has four adult children. From Conna in County Cork, he now lives in Malahide near Dublin.